WHERE
THE HELL IS
GOD?

Richard Leonard, SJ

FOREWORD BY
James Martin, SJ

HiddenSpring

Unless otherwise noted, the scripture quotations outlined herein are from the New Revised Standard Version Bible, copyright © 1989 by the Division of Christian Education of the National Council of Churches of Christ in the United States of America. Used by permission.

Cover design by Joy Taylor
Book design by Lynn Else

Library of Congress Cataloging-in-Publication Data

Leonard, Richard, 1963—
     Where the hell is God? / Richard Leonard.
          p. cm.
     Includes bibliographical references (p.   ).
     ISBN 978-1-58768-060-1 (alk. paper)
     1. Suffering—Religious aspects—Christianity. I. Title.
     BV4909.L47 2010
     248.8´6—dc22

                                                              2010010295

Published by HiddenSpring
An imprint of Paulist Press
997 Macarthur Boulevard
Mahwah, New Jersey 07430

www.paulistpress.com

Printed and bound in the
United States of America

CONTENTS

"This brilliant work by a gifted priest is one of the best books you will ever read on the question of suffering—in other words, one of the best books you will ever read on the spiritual life. Richard Leonard, a Jesuit priest and author whose family has known intense suffering, gently invites readers to confront the important questions that every believer will face one day. Wise, insightful, pastoral, original, and experienced—and never settling for easy answers—Father Leonard is the compassionate guide that all of us wish we had in times of pain. This profound book is for anyone who will face suffering in life—that is, everyone."

—James Martin, SJ, author of *The Jesuit Guide to Almost Everything*

"I found myself mentally cheering as I turned each page."

—Janet Moyle, *Catholic Voice* (Australia)

"This book is meant to be read slowly, over and over again....It presents a self-assured man in his own life tackling some of the hardest questions.... It never settles for easy answers."

—Kevin Ryan, *The Catholic Leader*

"A thoughtful book and one that bears the mark of experience, reading, and personal reflection."

—Andrew Hamilton, *Madonna*

"*Where the Hell Is God?* demolishes some of the answers that have taken up quarters in many, if not most, Christians' minds and hearts in regard to finding God in suffering. You will cringe when you realize what some of these 'answers' imply about God. God must be very happy with his friend Richard's attempt to understand and embrace him."

—William A. Barry, SJ

"An explosive and progressive message in a small wrapper, Leonard's book may frustrate Catholic and non-Catholic conservatives, but it will be a tonic for liberal Christians and seekers of all faiths."

—*Library Journal*

FOREWORD
James Martin, SJ

I have been waiting for years to read a book like this.

It is not a stretch to say that *Where the Hell Is God?* may change the way you look at your life. It is a book, as Richard Leonard says early on, that is not meant as an academic treatise on the theology of suffering, but as a heartfelt invitation to the person who has known suffering in life—that is to say, everyone.

My friend Richard Leonard is one of the best Jesuits I know. Learned, articulate, compassionate, and at times extremely funny, he is also one of the hardest working. Besides living an exceedingly busy life as a priest (with all the sacramental ministries that this entails), he is also a teacher, a writer, and a lecturer. Those who know him best as a teacher might be surprised to see how gifted a homilist he is during a crowded Sunday Mass. Those who know him best as a priest might be surprised to discover with what facility he writes about his particular area of academic expertise, the cinema. (Yes, like many Jesuit scholars, he has a PhD.) Those who know his academic work might be surprised to find out what a lively lecturer he is, ever in demand—from Melbourne to London to Rome to Los Angeles—to speak on a wide variety of topics.

But there is one thing that most people would not know, and that is his family's deep experience with suffering, which you will soon read about. That suffering—shocking, confusing, and intense—changed his family and changed Richard. Reading his reflections on that chapter of his life will change you.

WHERE THE HELL IS GOD?

Does that last sentence seem like an overstatement? It's not. For his new book explores the timeless question of "Why do we suffer?" but it does so in a unique way.

Most treatments of this difficult topic adopt one of two approaches. The first approach is from the theological standpoint, which is typically written by a theologian. Various perspectives from the Old and New Testaments are carefully weighed, and the age-old question of how a good God could allow suffering is thoughtfully considered in light of the writings of Christian saints and theologians. The second approach is from experience, which is typically written by someone who comes from outside the academic world. A person describes in detail his or her own story of personal suffering, or the suffering of a loved one, reflects on what has been learned, and provides insights and lessons for the reader. *Where the Hell Is God?* seamlessly *combines* these two approaches, for Richard is not only a gifted theologian but also someone with a life-altering experience of suffering.

You'll soon see that he also rejects "easy" answers, those banalities imposed upon the sufferer by otherwise well-meaning believers that often do more harm than good. Even devout believers recoil, and should recoil, in the face of pat responses to the immense mystery of suffering.

When my grandmother was in a nursing home, for example, one of her fellow residents was an elderly Catholic sister who was in a great deal of pain. One day, the sister's religious superior came to visit the ailing nun.

"Oh, I'm in so much pain," she said to her superior.

"Just think of Jesus on the Cross," replied the superior.

"Jesus was only on the Cross for three hours," she said sadly.

While the sister might have eventually found solace in the companionship of a Jesus who knew suffering, her superior's glib answer was unhelpful at best.

Richard Leonard knows that while there is truth in many of the traditional perspectives, every believer needs to explore the mystery of suffering for *himself or herself*, and to find personal meaning in the midst of pain, in companionship with the God who suffers alongside us. And this is what he helps readers to do in this brilliant new book. In his own frank and faithful grappling with suffering, in his own fearless plunge into the traditional perspectives on suffering, he leads us through the dark valleys and into a place of light.

Where the hell is God? Right here, in the pages of this book, which will help you find God even in the most difficult passages of your life.

JAMES MARTIN, SJ, is the author of *My Life with the Saints*, *Becoming Who You Are*, and *The Jesuit Guide to (Almost) Everything*.

PREFACE

Most philosophical or theological books on the topic of where or how God can be found in human suffering tend to be fairly academic. I have found them to be immensely important, even when I have disagreed with their arguments or conclusions. I have even found the intellectual distance they establish to be somehow helpful in dissecting an anything but distant inquiry.

Although I hope this book is intelligent, it is not meant for the academy. I will not be rehashing the many sides of the venerable arguments in the intellectual inquiry we now call theodicy. This book comes out of experience, of me grappling with a family tragedy that forced me to confront some fundamental questions about holding to my belief in a loving God in the face of evil. I do not want to claim too much for this accessible work. It is squarely in the area of what is called speculative theology. Over the centuries, greater minds than mine have applied themselves to these questions and have come to different conclusions about them. I am happy for that. The problem is that when I most needed their insights, I found their answers inadequate. I am not blaming them. The vast majority of them did not have the benefit of contemporary biblical studies, theology, science, and psychology to lend a hand.

The church knows, too, that it cannot be definitive about these matters because on this side of the grave, we just do not know where or how God fits in regard to the suffering of the world. Therefore, I make no greater claim for my work that has helped me hold on to faith in a loving God as I walked through the "valley of tears" and in the "shadow of death."

Maybe the best way to venture forth into this territory is through a story. As Holocaust survivor Elie Wiesel says, "You want to know about the kingdom of night? There is no way to describe the kingdom of night. But let me tell you a story...You want to know about the condition of the human heart? There is no way to describe the condition of the human heart. But let me tell you a story...You want a description of the indescribable? There is no way to describe the indescribable. But let me tell you a story."

So let me start with a story.

At dawn on the morning of my 25th birthday, the Jesuit superior of the house I was then in roused me from my bed to tell me that my mother was on the phone. I do not come from a very demonstrative family. We do not call each other at dawn on birthdays, but as soon as I heard Mum's voice, I knew this was not a happy birthday call. "Your sister has had a car accident, and I have to get to Darwin immediately. I am hoping you might come with me." My sister, Tracey, had completed her nursing studies straight after school and within months was in Calcutta nursing at Kalighat Home for the Dying, Mother Teresa's first foundation. She had returned home after six months to care for my mother, who was not well, but later returned to India. Eighteen months later, the Indian government refused to renew her visa because she was a volunteer, so she returned to Australia and got a job working with the Sisters of Our Lady of Sacred Heart in running a health center for the Aboriginal people at what was then called Port Keats, but now goes by its traditional name, Wadeye. She was young, full of life, and very capable. She was enlivened by the community at Port Keats as much as she had been by India.

The day before my birthday, Tracey found herself relieving the local nurse in another outback town, Adelaide River, a small, white, and Aboriginal community about one hour south of Darwin, the capital city of the Northern Territory. What happens next is Tracey's story, so I will let her tell it from her book, *The Full Catastrophe.*

"...It is near the end of my time in Adelaide River that I drive over to Port Keats for the weekend. I take Margaret, the wife of the plumber, and her three children with me, as her car won't be able to cope with the dirt roads. We have a wonderful weekend and are just outside Adelaide River on our return journey, when the engine gives a cough and dies. Fortunately, two vehicles come along shortly after we stop, and they offer to give us a tow into town.

"We are all hooked up and on our way, but before I realize what's happening, I find myself driving over the tow rope and my car veering off to the left. I grip the steering wheel to cushion the impact of a small tree looming in front of me, and the next thing I know, the entire car has rolled over, leaving me unsure whether I'm up or down. I cannot move a muscle and feel as if the entire roof of the car is pressing down on my head. My mouth and brain still work, though, and once I have ascertained the children are fine and Margaret is not badly hurt, I feel a great sense of relief. Our Good Samaritans are in a great state of anxiety; and one of them leans down to tell me that they'll go to Adelaide River and get the nurse. 'I *am* the f****** nurse,' I reply, and direct him to the house to which the regular nurse has just returned.

"Many hours later and with police, ambulance, and the nurse in attendance, I am freed from my metal entanglements. All I can feel is the most excruciating pain in my neck. They lay me on the ground, apply a neck brace, and then transfer me to a stretcher in the ambulance. One look at the worried faces of the people around me is enough to send my spirits plummeting. I have been conscious throughout this ordeal, and my brain knows that I can't feel anything below my shoulders, but the rest of my body is resisting this information.

"The trip to Darwin is agonizingly slow, as the ambulance crew keep stopping every twenty minutes to check my vital signs. I threaten death if they stop the vehicle once more, as the pain in my neck with every stop and start movement is unbearable. My other great concern is a stabbing pain at the back of my head and a very real sensation that ants are biting my scalp. It takes a little time to convince the ambulance attendant that I'm not suffering from head injuries and am completely serious in my complaint. Determined to shut me up, she starts combing through my hair where, much to her surprise, she discovers several large green ants. The reason for the pain in the back of my head turns out to be a sharp piece of twig. We hasten to Darwin without further incident, and I lie back on the stretcher and hope that this is all some horrible nightmare.

"I have the staff contact a friend of mine in Darwin to whom I entrust the job of ringing my mother and breaking the news."

Jill rang my mother around 1:30 a.m. to say Tracey had been in an accident, and while they were unaware of the extent of her injuries, Mother should come. Now, the next bit of the story is a "mother moment." My mother was widowed when she was 32. My father died of a massive stroke at the age of 36, and my mother then was a single parent to my brother, who was seven, my sister, who was five, and me, age two. Mum, who was living on her own at the time, decided that rather than wake up Peter and me, she thought it better that the two of us get a good night's sleep because there was nothing any of us could do until dawn. Mum rang no one. She sat there drinking cups of coffee and smoking cigarettes until dawn.

By 9:00 a.m., Mum and I were on a plane to Darwin. If you have ever touched tragedy in your own life, you will empathize with the denial that both of us went into—we found everything on that plane journey hysterically funny. We both laughed that on arrival, Tracey would be sitting up in bed and having a steak and a beer, laughing at us for being so melodramatic. Such a happy ending was not to be.

On arrival there were so many veiled and habited nuns at the airport, I thought the pope must be in the next plane. "The doctors will tell you everything when we get there." We were ushered into where Tracey was, and there was the long sheet pulled up to her chin. She had her arms out on extension boards at the side of the bed, and there were two huge spikes buried into her skull with weights at the back of the bed holding her head in place. I have never been able to look at a crucifix in the same way since.

My mother became very clinical and started asking Tracey what she could move. With two big tears just silently dropping down the side of her head, my sister simply said, "I'm a bloody quad, Mum. I have dislocated the 5th cervical vertebrae and fractured the 6th and 7th vertebrae. This is as bad as it gets."

Fight and flight are two common reactions to shock. We chose the latter. Tracey says she does not know between my mother and me who beat whom to get out of the door first. The pastoral care sister put us in a room on our own. I sat at a desk, and for one of the first times in my life I was speechless. My mother started pacing the floor. She was angry. It was like one of the lioness's cubs had been left for dead and she was going to get who was responsible for it. As she paced, my mother started asking a series of questions:

How could God do this to Tracey?

How could God do this to us?

What more does God want from me in this life?

And most hauntingly of all,

Where the hell is God?

These were rhetorical questions, but I was a Jesuit. God was my game, so I ventured an answer. But every time I went to speak, my mother bit off my head. At these times we often lash out at the ones who are closest to us. I wanted to remind my mother that I was one of the cubs too!

Still, I plucked up my courage and had, arguably, the most painful and important theological discussion I will ever have in my life. I told my mother that if anyone can prove to me that God sat in heaven last night and thought, "I need another quadriplegic, and Tracey will do, so let's set up a car accident to get that happening"—if this was God's active will—then I am leaving the priesthood, the Jesuits, and the church. I don't know that God, I don't want to serve that God, and I don't want to be that God's representative in the world. So my mother came back at me, "So where is God, then?" And I gently said, "I think God is as devastated as we are right now that a generous, selfless girl, who went all over the world looking after the poor, is now the poorest person we know." It had nothing to do with money. I did not have to choose between a God of love and a God who does cruel things to us. Like the God who groans with loss in Isaiah and Jesus who weeps at his best friend's tomb in John 11, God was not standing outside our pain, but was our companion within it, holding us in his arms, sharing in our grief and pain.

In the months that followed, I got some of the most appalling and frightening letters from some of the best Christians I knew. A few wrote, "Tracey must have done something to deeply offend God, so she had to be punished here on earth, for God will not be mocked!" They went on, "the only way to know peace with God now is to accept his will." They actually believe that God gets us. I have discovered since 1988 that this theology is far more common than I would have ever imagined. I have met people with cancer, couples with fertility problems, and parents who have lost a child in death who have asked me what they ever did to deserve the curse under which they think God has placed them. I want to weep just thinking about them.

Others wrote, "Tracey's suffering is sending up glorious building blocks to heaven for her mansion there when she dies." This is what is usually called "pie-in-the-sky-when-you-die theology." I did not know that in heaven, in the many rooms of the Father's house, there are first, business, and economy class suites. And if that's so, then heaven will be the first counter in my life where I will not be looking for an upgrade! For if to get from the shantytown just inside the pearly gates to the best celestial suburb means being washed, fed, turned, toileted, and clothed every day for over twenty years now, then I cannot pay the price for the move across town. I think very few people could.

Finally, there were scores of letters and cards that said, "Your family is really very blessed, because God only sends the biggest crosses to those who can bear them." I always like how some people who are not receiving that particular blessing can see it so clearly in other people's suffering. But let us think about this line a little more. We hear it often. If this line is true, then we should all be on our knees morning, noon, and night with only one prayer: "I am a wimp. I am a wimp. I am a wimp, O God. Do not consider me strong." Because if this theology is true and God thinks you are strong, you are going to be blessed with a big cross.

Added to these responses were good people who were trying to be comforting, and so gave out the usual trio of replies in the face of bad news: "It's all a mystery"; "My ways are not your ways"; and "Only in heaven will we find out God's plan." There is a truth in each of these statements, but I am not at all convinced that they are baldly true in the way some people mean them. They are often used by good people to say something they hope will be comforting. It did not have that effect on me. For example, while it is absolutely true that God's ways and thoughts are infinitely greater than anything we can hope or imagine, invoking Isaiah 55 in the midst of people's suffering tends to place God outside our human drama, as an all-knowing and yet uncaring observer to the action of our lives. Yet, I think one of the greatest points of the incarnation, of God becoming one with us in Jesus Christ, is precisely that God wants to reveal his ways and thoughts, wants to be known, especially in regard to the moments when we are sometimes given to the greatest despair. The life, death, and resurrection of Jesus show us that God has grafted himself onto human history in the most intimate of ways. We do not believe and love an aloof being who revels in mystery and goes AWOL when the action turns tough in our lives. The incarnation surely shows us that God is committed to being a participant in the human adventure in all its complexity and pain.

So I am very grateful to the correspondents who wrote to me after my sister's accident. They have alerted me to how often we hear some terrible theology that does not draw us to God in the worst moments of our lives. It alienates us. It alienated me for a while from believing in a God who wants us to have an intelligent discussion about the complexities of where and how the divine presence fits into our fragile and human world. So here are my seven steps to spiritual sanity when we are tempted and we give in to the temptation to ask, "Where the hell is God?"

1. God does not directly send pain, suffering, and disease. God does not punish us.
2. God does not send accidents to teach us things, though we can learn from them.
3. God does not will earthquakes, floods, droughts, or other natural disasters. Prayer asks God to change us to change the world.
4. God's will is more in the big picture than in the small.
5. God did not *need* the blood of Jesus. Jesus did not just come "to die," but God used his death to announce the end to death.
6. God has created a world that is less than perfect, and in which suffering, disease, and pain are realities; otherwise, it would be heaven. Some of these problems we now create for ourselves and blame God.
7. God does not kill us off.

CHAPTER ONE

God is not out to get us.

God does not directly send or will pain, death, suffering, and disease. God does not punish us with bad things.

I have come to see that some people believe in a tyrannical God. The usual modern idea about human tyrants is that they are absolute rulers who maintain their power through fear and death, torture and oppression. Understandably, most of the population do not take on the tyrant, not only because of their fear, but also because their primary task is just to try and survive the regime.

The people who wrote to me and suggested that my sister had to be punished by God for her offenses or as a way to merit heaven, believe in a tyrannical God. Tracey remains one of the finest and most generous people I know. The idea that life is about surviving the regime is much more alive and well in the popular imagination than we may like to accept. It shows its ugly head when we do or say something we should not have and then stub our toe. We can think that God is giving us an immediate wake-up call. This idea holds that God tolerates bad behavior up to a point, but then has to stop the nonsense by reminding us who is boss. Toes are one thing, quadriplegia is quite another.

It lurks behind those scandalous chain letters that masquerade as "prayer guides" to St. Jude, "hope of the hopeless," where if we follow all their absurd instructions precisely, then God will grant our petition. If our prayers are not answered, then it follows that we must have missed a step, and sometimes the chain letter says that any deviation from the prescription will be punished by God's wrath. Most of us do not take these things seriously; nor should we, given that it reduces God to being a ringmaster of the earthly circus, cracking the divine whip as we jump through the necessary hoops. And in the oddest contradictions, it can also mean that we believe that God will jump and act in our favor when we fulfill the requirements of the chain letter. For the record, we do not have to write out a prayer nine times and leave it in nine churches, or forward nine e-mails for God to listen to us, or for him to take our prayers seriously.

Some people say that the idea that God directly sends or wills pain, death, suffering, and disease is the "Old Testament image of God." While we all know there are parts of the Old Testament that reinforce such an image—babies' heads being bashed against the rocks, the enemy being smitten, and God killing off the firstborn sons of an entire nation—taken as a whole and with cultural intelligence and care, the Old Testament is a long and complex love song about salvation, and how God wants us to live, not die.

God as a tyrant is a fearful, neat solution to the deep pain within some people's lives. Suffering has to come from somewhere, and when innocent people suffer, others conclude that the pain was sent directly by God. I use the word *directly* here advisedly. I believe that God has to take some responsibility for the moral and physical evil in the world, but only "indirectly." I imagine God could have set in motion a world that is better than this one, but I cannot be sure of that. Given that God wanted to give us the gift of free will, even to the point where we can reject God, and that as a result of this freedom we can make destructive choices, maybe this world is as good as it gets. In any case, we have to deal with the world as it is.

2

So I reject that God is an absolute ruler who maintains power through fear and death, torture, and oppression, primarily because I cannot see this in the person and work of Jesus, but also because I could not truly love such a God. Inverting St. John's line in 1 John 1, "true fear drives out love." I want to have "fear of the Lord" in its most traditional sense of being reverent before God, being in awe of God's presence and creation, but I also want to return the love of God with an offering of love. And to do so I cannot be frightened.

It would be impossible, I believe, for any of us to truly love a God whom we honestly believed kills our babies, sends us breast cancer, makes us infertile, and sets up car accidents to even up the score. Even on its own terms, this God looks like a small god, a petty tyrant who seems to be in need of anger management class where he might learn how to channel all that strong angry emotion into creation, not destruction. Furthermore, if God were into sending evil upon us, you might think he would start with the worst sinners, the real tyrants of our world, and leave the rest of us for later, but it never seems to go like that.

So how can I be so confident that God is not deadly by nature? First, in 1 John 1:5 we are told that "God is light and in him there is no darkness." I do not want to be accused of "proof texting"—that unfortunate religious disease from which some Christians suffer, where they think a single scriptural text that seems to back up their argument is the last word on the topic. Taken in context, 1 John 1:5 is actually a sermon about the light of God's love shining in and through Jesus. Probably written for the church at Ephesus in the latter part of the first century, it seems to be a rebuttal of a heresy around at the time, that Jesus was more a spirit than one enfleshed. John is at pains to say that Jesus is God's light in the world in and through his sacrificial love for us, and that those of us who want to walk in this light must love others as Jesus loved us.

3

In this context, we can see how cancer, car accidents, and the death of children, husbands, and anyone we love are dark things that cannot have a place within God. They cannot be part of his arsenal of weapons to test us out, and to inflict pain on us to see how we cope. We are told repeatedly by Paul and other New Testament authors that death and destruction are manifestations of disorder, so they cannot be part of light itself, and of pure love. The sort of thinking that suggests that darkness does in fact dwell in God has made its way into our ordinary conversation. Think of how many times we have heard a phrase like, "Well, that was the hand I was dealt, so now I have to get on with it." Sometimes "the hand" includes the death of a loved one, growing up in a violent home, or suffering from a disease. The metaphor of life as a card game has its limitations, in any case, but I am interested in who Christians may think is doing the dealing when they use this phrase. In almost all cases it is God, here seen to be actively dealing a rough hand to unsuspecting and unfortunate players at life's table of chance. If we must use this metaphor, then at least we might be able to say that life is the dealer of the hand and that it is chancier than any of us might be prepared to contemplate. The good news is that, rather than see God in the dealer's seat, he is on our side, in every sense of that phrase, accompanying us in the game.

The second reason I am so confident that God is not deadly by nature is that we are mindful of the nature and actions of Jesus. Regardless of the varied images of God in the Old Testament, we are people of the new covenant and as a result of that we interpret the God of the Old Testament in the light of the New Testament. In the Gospels we see that God's Word and Wisdom made flesh in Jesus Christ is all about life, not death, construction, not destruction, heal-ing, not pain. And there is not a page of the New Testament upon which we can read about Jesus taking anything away from anyone.

4

No one went to him with one bad leg and had to be carried away because he took off the other one for good measure. He may have even gotten justifiably angry with the money sellers in the temple, where we are told he drove them out, but we are not told that he whipped them senseless. Jesus certainly confronted the Pharisees, Sadducees, Zealots, and Teachers of the Law, but he was never vengeful. He did not have them rubbed out for their trouble. Not even the Romans, who were then the enemies of Israel, were treated with anything but respect, and one was even praised for his great faith. Even today, Christ confronts, challenges, and tells us we have to carry our cross and bear our burdens, but that is a vastly different thing from saying the Father, Son, and Spirit send the crosses to us and lay the burdens on us in the first place.

Let me underline again that as Christians, we do not believe that when Jesus acted in a loving and compassionate way, he was just putting on a good show, indeed a human face, for a vengeful, nasty Father in heaven. In fact, we hold that to see Jesus in action is to see God definitively in action, because "I can do nothing on my own" and "the Father and I are one." So if Jesus was not into hurting us, then neither is God.

This is not to suggest that we should run away from those tough New Testament texts about judgment and justice. I passionately believe in God's justice. Anyone who takes free will seriously has to. But it is good to make a distinction between judgment and condemnation. These days, we often hear people say "we should not judge." Some people even think being nonjudgmental is a particularly Christian trait because, they claim, "Jesus did not judge anyone." I do not have a clue what Gospel they are reading, but it is not Matthew, Mark, Luke, or John. Their assertion is a mistake on almost every level. When we hear people say "don't judge," we can assume they are really saying "don't condemn," but there is a world of difference between judging and condemning. To judge is to make an assessment. To condemn is to damn. There is not a page of the New Testament where Jesus is not judging people's behavior, but he never condemns them. The woman taken in adultery in John 8 is among the most famous of stories in this regard, "Woman, where are they? Has no one condemned you?" She said, "No one, sir." And Jesus said, "Neither do I condemn you. Go your way, and from now on do not sin again." Allied to this story is that the Christian tradition holds that one of the seven gifts of the Holy Spirit is right judgment. It seems strange that she would give us this gift as if we were never meant to exercise it.

It is in this light of Jesus judging but not condemning, that I read those often apocalyptic texts about God's justice. I believe that, if we feel condemned for what we have done and said, then it's because we have condemned ourselves, not because God is out to get us. John tells us that even when we find ourselves lost in the darkness of our most destructive behavior, the saving love of Christ is always available to us, inviting us to come out of the darkness into his light. Condemnation may be the prerogative of God alone, who sees all, knows all, and loves all, but given the example of Jesus, then God's judgment will be full of compassion because all will be laid bare, even every context and reason for our bad behavior.

I want to end this chapter with an application of how wrong we are to hold on to the idea that God directly sends pain and death and uses disease to punish us in this life.

In 1986, I heard an evangelical preacher say that God sent HIV/AIDS to punish gay people for their sins. Indeed, he claimed, God was killing them because they were an abomination. This may not have been said as explicitly by other church leaders and believers, but it was expressed in more moderate tones, and is held by some Christians to this day. This sort of commentary is, of course, more revealing of the speaker than it is of God. It would seem for these people that God's love and goodness has its limits, and homosexuality exhausts God's patience. This line was wrong then and it is wrong now, not only because there is no one who is beyond God's love and compassion, but because there is ample evidence in the Bible that God has a particular love for those rejected and despised by any society and who are pushed to its fringes. Our God seems to like the margins best of all. In this context, it would be a total denial of the biblical witness to hold that God not only dislikes those who, for a variety of reasons, are most in need of his presence, but that he is so angry with them that he uses disease to do away with them. This is the God of the Nazis.

But what has happened since 1986 really throws into relief the absurdity of the assertion in the first place. Tragically and scandalously, the United Nation now reports that 49 percent of all people in the world now living with HIV/AIDS are sub-Saharan African women and children. Most of these women were infected by heterosexual transmission, or passed the infection onto their child while in their womb. What did they ever do to be "punished" in this way, or are they just collateral damage in God's war against the gay community? If so, God's blood lust knows no bounds. The body count is rising.

There is a huge difference between God permitting evil and God perpetrating such acts on us. We need to stare down those who promote and support an image of God as a tyrant. In its place, let us cling to God, in whom there is no darkness, made visible in Christ Jesus who subdues tyranny in all its forms, and who not only accompanies us through pain, death, suffering, and disease, but even seeks us out when we are most lost, and guides us home.

CHAPTER TWO

*We grow through pain, but it is
not sent to make us grow.*

God does not send accidents to teach us things, though we can learn
from them.

When my mother and I were standing in that hospital room, there
was no way of knowing how much all our lives were about to
change—most of all, and most heartbreakingly, for my sister. Her
words tell her story, again.

"I am now a quadriplegic, and I don't know if I'll ever be able
to accept it.

"Four days after the accident, I'm transferred to the Spinal
Injuries Unit at the Princess Alexandra Hospital in Brisbane. This
is where reality really kicks in. I now have two metal tongs drilled
into my skull, and these are joined by a U-shaped piece of metal to
a rope and pulley attached to the head of the bed. The rope extends
down to a bag of weights, which acts as traction against my broken
bones. My neck is four times its normal size and looks like something out of a horror movie. Apart from this, all I have to show for
the extent of damage to my body is a minuscule graze on my head.

"The doctors here are specialists in spinal injuries, and they
have the standard talk down pat. I have a complete spinal cord
injury at cervical 6/7, and as a result have lost all feeling and
movement from the chest down, including bladder and bowel. I

have lost feeling and movement in some of my arm muscles and completely in my hands....

"At least a hundred times a day I run a mental inventory of what I can feel and move. I concentrate my entire being and run a check on my body from my toes to my head. This process is an emotional rollercoaster of hope and devastation, but is like a drug that I can't live without. I can feel my head and shoulders, and this 10 percent of my body screams for 100 percent of my attention. A simple task such as blowing a blocked nose requires help from another person and never achieves a satisfactory result. An itchy scalp seems to be my constant companion, and at times I feel like I'm lying on an ants' nest. My most dreaded experience is that when a lone mosquito decides to call; its uniquely piercing scream reverberates in my head. On many occasions my arm has risen in a reflex motion to fight off my buzzing nemesis, only to come crashing down on my metal skull attachments, thus further enhancing the pain experience. I eventually learn, in some Pavlovian fashion, that some inconveniences are better left ignored.

"The other significant facet of life attached to a bed is time. There is far too much time to think. The usual questions of 'Why?' and 'What if?' dominate my thinking. For some unknown reason, I've been anointed three times since my accident. It is called 'the blessing of the sick.' It is not your final send-off, but a fairly normal response to catastrophe in Catholic circles. I have also had the dubious honor of hearing every religious cliché in the book regarding suffering and God's plan. This is another one of the consequences of immobility—the inability to escape unwanted visitors...

"I think about all the people I have met and nursed over the years and the hundreds I have seen die. I do not fear death and in many ways would welcome it. Many times when I'm rewriting history, I make sure that the accident is a fatal one. This is also fruitless thinking but comforting in its own strange way. The big surprise in my many thinking sessions is the number of people I wouldn't trade places with. I now have some appreciation for the physical deformity of the lepers, but even though many of them are mobile, I couldn't bring myself to swap quadriplegia for leprosy. Another group that receives a negative response is the destitute of Calcutta. The mere fact of surviving is not life for me. The last group is the Aborigines. I don't think I could live in this society as a black person without committing violence against all the little discriminations, let alone the major ones. I'm much safer in a wheelchair, and so is the Aboriginal cause.

"Unwittingly, the prisoners of the local Boggo Road jail provide not only entertainment but inspiration for us inhabitants of the Spinal Unit. Whenever they stage a break-out, we line the veranda and cheer them on. They have a better chance of escaping their bars than we do, and while they are not always successful, at least they have a go at escaping. This attitude opens a small window in my mind. Life will go on and maybe my adventures are not finished yet."

The "adventure" was just beginning. We do not need to blame God directly for causing our suffering for us to turn it around and harness it for good. The human search for meaning is a powerful instinct. Tracey's accident, however, was meaningless in itself. It was a random event, an intersection of the wrong time and the wrong place and the worst outcome. I say the worst outcome quite deliberately because on the day after the accident, when we arrived in Darwin, had the doctors said to us, "While you were flying up here your daughter and sister died of her injuries, but we want you to know that had she lived, she would have been a quadriplegic," we would have taken death as some sort of tragic comfort. "Who could ever imagine Tracey, of all people, being a quad?" "How would she have coped?" "How would we have coped?" These are the sorts of questions I can imagine I would have asked in the midst of my despair and grief.

But the adventure was just beginning for all of us. Although it has haunted me ever since, I am the least affected person in my family by my sister's accident. I live away from the town and state in which the rest of my clan lives. My mother's life has changed completely. At 56, and for decades since, she has become an utterly dedicated full-time caregiver. My brother, Peter, his wife, and children live near our family home, and they have always been there for my sister. Tracey did not proceed with her then engagement to be married. There were several times, early on, when she asked us to euthanize her. We have seen the loyalty of some outstanding friends and family.

It was mostly out of sheer boredom, I think, but two years after her accident, Tracey decided to write up the stories of her life in Calcutta. Only a mother could have stored away in the loft every single letter that Tracey wrote from India over the years. They became the basis upon which she sat for hours hitting the keyboard with extensions on her two index fingers, weaving the stories into a longer narrative. It was slow work. By the end of that year there were 11 pages to read. She sent them to me for some feedback, "from your literary mates." One of my friends was the celebrated Australian novelist, Thea Astley. Her brother, Philip, was a Jesuit. Thea may have been a sophisticated writer, with Australia's highest literary awards to prove it, but her speech was direct and earthy. She rang me up and said, "Your sister is a bloody good storyteller isn't she. She has the basis of a decent book here." I put the two plain-spoken women in contact with each other, and they became firm friends, as I suspected they would. Computers have revolutionized disability, and within that year Tracey had a voice-activated program to which she could dictate. With Thea's mentoring in the background, four years later *The Full Catastrophe* was published, regaling the reader with stories of her life in Calcutta and the Northern Territory. Shortlisted in a few literary competitions that year for best new work, its biggest impact has been on adventurous young people, would-be volunteers, and other paraplegics and quadriplegics.

So in some measure, Tracey turned around a meaningless accident and was generous with what she still had left to offer—her story, humor, wisdom, and experience. Through God's grace, the rest of us have learned a lot, too, about the big lessons regarding ourselves, one another, and the precariousness of life. But I have also learned from this accident to be grateful when I bound up stairs two at a time, feed myself, stand in the shower unaided, or actually use the toilet on my own. At these deeply ordinary human moments, I thank God, because I have discovered that even the lavatory can be a house of prayer.

I have been an incredibly active person all my life, but several years ago a Jesuit superior of mine challenged me about my busy lifestyle. "Why are you on the move all the time?" he asked. Without even thinking, I looked at him, welled up with tears and said, "Because I can."

One of the greatest lessons all my family has painfully acquired over the time is coping with the restrictions disabled people have to bear. I am the one who will confront you in the parking lot if I see you alight ably from a car with no "disability" sticker when it is parked in the disability parking place because it is the closest one to the store. There are also hotels with disability bathrooms that no seriously disabled person could access. Our family has been to expensive restaurants that charge my sister the same price for dining in their establishment, with the only disabled access being the service elevator with the cabbages, and then through the pot washing area in the kitchen. There are the cold temperatures of most public buildings, the way people yell in exaggerated voices at people they don't know in wheelchairs, presuming them to be mentally disabled and hearing impaired, as well as some contemporary architects who like to ward off skateboarders with cobbled pavements. Try going over those in a wheelchair.

The greatest gift this searing experience has given me, however, is to have a greater empathy for anyone who is devastated in grief or who feels abandoned by life or God. I have touched that moment, and I have asked, on more than one occasion, "Where the hell is God?" That moment has irrevocably changed my ministry as a priest for the better.

Given that, with God's power and love, good can come out of disasters, this in no way changes the nature of the terrible event in the first place. It does not become God's will that we grow as a result of a shocking event. If that were true, then this could be argued: because our study of genetics has benefited significantly from the evil experiments on 1,500 pairs of twins at the hands of the Nazi doctor Josef Mengele, then the good application of his findings to the later mapping of the human genome and cures that may come of this, means that God wanted these experiments to happen so that good would ultimately arise out of evil. I do not know anyone who argues this case in this way. In fact, there is understandable ethical disquiet in some sections of the scientific community about using experimental results acquired in evil circumstances.

This principle of revising the horror of terrible events in the face of later and good developments, however, happens all the time on a more personal and domestic level. People will say, "Well, given all the good that has happened since, now I know why God took my husband or baby, or I got breast cancer, or that accident occurred." Rather, I think spiritual sanity rests in seeing that every moment of every day God does what he did on Good Friday, not to allow evil, death, and destruction to have the last word, but to ennoble humanity with an extraordinary resilience, and through the power of amazing grace, to enable us to make the most of even the worst situations and let light and life have the last word. Easter Sunday is God's response to Good Friday: life out of death.

CHAPTER THREE

And now let's cross to God the Weatherman.
Can we stop praying for rain?

God does not will earthquakes, floods, droughts, or other natural disasters.

Philosophers have traditionally made helpful distinctions between different types of evil: physical, moral, and metaphysical, to name the big three. Physical evil is the one we have been considering so far, where even without an evil intention, unlike a murder, a bad thing happens to our person, or living situation, or personal and social freedom. Most people wonder where God is in physical evil.

Moral evil is the one we have probably heard about more than any other form. This is the evil that results from human choices and actions. In Christian theology, personal culpability for the moral evil I may choose, and social culpability, for that matter, hinge on how free, deliberate, and knowing I am in regard to the choices I make. This is where we talk of sin, informed conscience, and morality. There are overlaps between physical and moral evil. While moral evil may have a very real physical outcome, the cause of it is not in the external world, which we cannot control, but in the process of human decision making, which we can control.

Moral codes do not have to be religious. Every human group establishes boundaries for behavior, decision making, and punishment for known transgressors. All civil laws carry within them an agreed basic moral code, and many people who profess no religious faith have a highly developed secular and humanistic moral frame of reference within which they live their lives. The primary function of religion and morality is not to simply explain the how of living, but to place morality in the context of the why of it, and, indeed, the where of it—where we came from, why we are here, and where we are going. Religion is not about morality per se; rather, and more importantly, it provides meaning and coherence for why we live the way we do.

Metaphysical evil is about the clash of good and evil on a more cosmic level. This is the stuff of myth in its richest sense, where humanity tries to grapple with how evil started, whether this world is the best one that could have been created, and why God seems to permit suffering. The stories of Adam and Eve, the Garden of Eden, and the Fall are possibly the most profound myths, using simple stories to explain the biggest questions. An explanation of one type of evil begs questions in the other categories, as we will now see.

Australia is currently living through the longest drought known to most of the population. It is heartbreaking to see rivers dry up, cattle and sheep needing to be slaughtered, and people leaving the farms their families have run for generations. The suicide rate has increased during the drought, the divorce rate has also gone up and, as people leave the area for work, small towns and communities have been dislocated and some are dying. Evil is a big word to describe the fallout from the drought, but only a person who has not been directly touched by it would think of it in less dramatic terms.

My problem with the drought has been with the response of religious leaders to it. For years now, in almost every church in Australia, we have been "praying for rain." In dioceses where the drought is acutely felt, the local bishop may even have held a

"Mass for rain" in the cathedral. On one level, this is entirely appropriate, stating as it symbolically does, that God wants to enter into every part of our lives and stands in solidarity with us in our joys and hopes, grief and anxieties. Even in a drought, God wants us to name what our needs are. These occasions are cries of the heart. They can be occasions for a liturgical lament, of a collective expression of communal pain. My concern arises because they are rarely couched in these terms, and they raise more questions about the role we think God is taking in the drought itself.

I was at Mass in a country cathedral when a well-educated bishop started preaching about the drought. He was wonderfully empathetic of his people on the land who were struggling. But when he said, "We have no idea why God has sent the drought to us, but we must both beg him for rain, and live lives worthy of his kindness," then I could see that physical and moral evil had met. I was astonished that this good man would link our lives with the weather. Theology did not seem to have come very far since the story of Noah in Genesis 6—9, except now God was teaching us something by withholding water, not sending it.

There is no question that both the Old and New Testaments and the tradition of the church urge persistent prayer for particular intentions, even for and against rain (Jas 5:17—18). The problem is that these ideas emerge from a prescientific people who thought that rain came from windows in the sky, which God opened and closed at will and whim. The dialogue between science and faith should also have an impact on the way we pray.

The first part of his sentence was particularly problematic. The bishop was not just articulating a traditional, but inadequate, position: "We have no idea why God has created a world where this sort of devastating drought is possible." He was going further, and so do many others. The idea that God was sitting in heaven actively sending a drought upon Australia makes me anxious. We cast God in the role of the great-meteorologist-in-the-sky all the time. Brides do this especially. I have lost count of how many brides, over whose wedding ceremonies I am presiding, have asked me to pray for a fine day. Except for the ease of the guests and the options a sunny day gives for a wedding photographer, I do not think it matters one iota whether there is hail, rain, or shine for a wedding, or any other significant day. I think God has greater problems to worry about, at least I hope so. Here my anxiety is two-fold. Christianity has sometimes been critical of animist religions where they hold elaborate ceremonies to get the gods of nature to do their bidding in relation to the weather. I cannot see much difference between the Hollywood cliché of a Chinook priest dancing around the totem pole asking the gods to "send rain, send rain, send rain" and a bishop having a "Mass for rain" in his cathedral. The same theology can be active in both circumstances—if we pray hard enough or long enough or change our lives, God will relent and send the rain we need. My problem is, what do we think God is doing in heaven? Is he sitting there saying, "No, I will not send rain, so go away, dry up, and die." Surely not! I do accept that we might gather for a Mass where we ask God to make us strong in the face of drought. The Catholic missal has Masses for all sorts of desperate occasions. These can be easily reclaimed as part of a liturgical lament where we gather to cry out in our need to the same God who is already present to us, aware of our need, and weeping with us. The psalmists were on to something powerful in this regard.

Let's be clear that we can and should pray about water, the earth, and the environment. If we are truly pro-life, it is inescapable that we have to be pro-planet as well. We might even have Masses where we ask for the grace to be the best stewards of creation that we can be, but this is a long way from the Mass for rain. This raises another vital point: what do we think we are doing when we enter into petitionary prayer—does prayer change God, change us, or change both? On the morning of December 26, 2004, there were two undersea earthquakes measuring between 9.1 and 9.3 on the Richter scale in the Indian Ocean, sending tsunamis toward the surrounding coastlines of Indonesia, Sri Lanka, India, and Thailand. It is estimated that nearly 283,100 people were killed that day. That night on Australian radio there was a show that was taking calls in relation to listeners' reaction to the day's terrible events. Almost all the callers were shocked and sympathetic. Many pledged to do what they could to support relief efforts. I was stunned when a caller claiming to be a "Christian preacher" said, "Well, you have to realize that these Muslims had it coming, and that when God says he will defend his people, he means it." This is the same sort of terrible theology that argued that 9/11 was sent by God as a punishment for sins, and a wake-up call for the United States to turn back to Christ.

Taking the caller's argument more seriously than it deserves, we have to wonder how he copes with the fact that the parts of Sri Lanka that were deluged that day were predominately Christian. It seems those tens of thousands of poor victims were collateral damage in God's bloody act of retribution.

So when our children ask, "Why did the tsunami happen?" I think it best if we just tell them the simple geophysical truth: "Because the earth shelf moved, setting off a big wave." If we want to elaborate the story a little, we might tell them one of the reasons so many people died that day was that, despite the fact that the poorer countries of the Indian Ocean Rim had been asking the wealthy countries of the world for some time to assist them in establishing a tsunami early warning system, this had not happened. If this system had been in place then, while loss of life was probably unavoidable, several hours of lag time between the earthquake and the tsunami reaching the coastlands would have meant mass evacuations and would have saved many lives. These countries have such a system now.

And why is there a drought? With all due respect to the good bishop, I do not believe God is actively sending it so that my prayerful begging may increase, or to teach me to clean up my act. By contrast, I think it may be that the earth's climate is in a long-term cyclical pattern, which we have not had the tools to measure or the records to read, until now. It could be due to solar flares over which we have no control. It might also be that in some of our countries, we have populated the wrong areas, grown the wrong crops, and not been good stewards of the earth locally and globally. The worst-case scenario is that it is a combination of these factors. In any case, we now know that the earth is much more fragile, and more balanced and finely tuned than we thought. It is evolving all the time, now, literally, groaning in an act of giving birth. As such, is this more precarious planet the best one God could have created? We do not know. It just is, and every day it provides us with challenges about how we see ourselves as part of the created order, working with all living things in partnership for the future of the world given into our care. God accompanies us, guides us, has instructed us about the consequences of greed and avarice, and not making better decisions when the consequences of stupid ones, even in regard to weather and climate, are staring us in the face.

So if I should not pray about rain or a fine day for my wedding, then why should I pray at all?

I think a good number of Christians do not actually pray to the God and Father of Jesus Christ, but to Zeus. Not that they are intending to pray to this pagan Greek god; it is just that their approach to prayer leads me to conclude that some people believe in a Zeus-like god, and not just because he was Olympus' resident meteorologist. In Greek mythology, Zeus was in charge of the skies and thunder, the king of all the gods, and the ruler of Olympus, the home of the gods. Zeus was not an easy god with whom to get along. Though he could be loving and kind, he was more famous for being moody and unpredictable. When his ire was raised, he killed, maimed, punished, and handed other gods and mortals over to be tortured in a variety of exotic ways. Life with Zeus was unpredictable. One of the lessons lesser gods and mortals learned quickly was that if you wanted a good deal out of life, then you had to stay on Zeus' good side. As with all the Greek gods, sacrifice and prayer were the usual offerings. In Zeus' case, however, slaughtered oxen, which were then an enormous economic unit, were offered. The hierarchy of sacrifices and the length of prayers seem to have been in relation to how much a petitioner wanted Zeus to listen to the plea, change his mind, or be kind to him or her. Tragically, there is some archeological evidence that people went as far as human sacrifice to appease this greatest of the gods.

Rightly, since the earliest centuries of the church, our God was different from the gods that had gone before—different from Zeus. Building on the foundation of Judaism, we proclaim that:

- God is one;
- God is eternal: will not burn out;
- God is immutable: does not change;
- God is self-existent: not caused by any other being, is the first cause;
- God is transcendent: we are made in God's likeness, not he in ours;
- God is omnipotent: all-powerful;
- God is omnipresent: all-present;
- God is omniscient: all-knowing;
- God is holy: perfect in love.

The traditional Christian doctrine of immutability holds that God, in his essence, is unchanging. By the way some people speak of God, we get the impression that they think God could change if he wanted to because he is all-powerful. God's unchanging nature is essential for the sake of our relationship with him and our sanity. This affects petitionary prayer.

I single out petitionary prayer, mindful that our prayer tends to follow the categories of the psalms. Apart from asking God for something, our prayer can also lament our situation, that is, cry out in anguish; it can give thanks and praise; affirm our trust and faith; sing of our salvation; and simply wait upon the presence of God.

It must be conceded, however, that the most common form of address from humanity to God, is asking for something to happen to someone somewhere. And I believe that all the sacrifices and prayers in the world cannot change God because that is the way God wants it.

So what does our petitionary prayer do? Why bother praying to a God who does not change? When we pray, we are asking our holy, loving, and unchanging God to change us, and thereby change the world. Unlike Zeus, the real Christian God cannot wake up in a bad mood today and is not unpredictable. It is near impossible to have a steady and loving relationship with a volatile human being, so how much more fraught would our relationship with God be if he were characterized by being random (in the classic sense of the word) or erratic? Jesus, the Word of the Father for the world, was strong and constant. And on the nature of God, the Apostle James says, "Every good and perfect gift is from above, coming down from the Father of the heavenly lights, who does not change like shifting shadows" (Jas 1:17).

This is a great relief in our life of faith and in our prayer. We do not have to be anxious about God's justified anger, at least in this life, and then fret about God killing, maiming, punishing, or tor-turing us. But you would be forgiven for thinking that by the way some people talk about God, and how some of us were taught to pray. It seemed that prayer was all about asking, or telling, God what to do, to change his mind, to send rain when he may not want to. I take the role of prayer so seriously in our lives that I want us to make sure we know whom we are praying to and what we can expect from the encounter. If God cannot change from our prayer, we can, and we should.

In theology, we talk about God pouring himself out in and through Jesus for the sake and salvation of the world. *Kenosis* is the fancy Greek term to describe this action and activity. God is spent in loving us and saving us at every moment of the day. He cannot do more in this regard. It is up to us to respond to this unearned and unmerited gift, and that's what prayer does. It invites his amazing grace to change, form, fashion, heal, and inspire us. This happens not only in our personal prayer, but also our public prayer. Liturgies in all their styles and forms are not about the power of a larger number calling on a changeable God to roll over on a partic-ular point. That would be a political rally. No, liturgy is where we join our personal prayer with the prayer of the assembled church, and the whole world, asking God to change us, so that we might more reflect his loving face and thereby transform the world.

Now, it might seem odd that I claim that God cannot or does not change nature, but can change the human heart. I do not believe, however, that God can change a human heart that does not want to change. Grace builds on nature; it does not obliterate it. We are seduced into changing by the grace of God, not forced to do it. There are enough examples of how good people make terri-ble choices and evil people do evil things for us to know that our freedom has been God's greatest and most risky gift to us.

If ever you want to know who a worshipping community is praying to and what they think prayer is about, listen to their prayers of the faithful, their "bidding" prayers. Most of the prayers ask God to do something in such a way that lets us off the hook. "Dear God, raise up the poor, bring peace, or feed the hungry." We know that God wants all these things to happen, and sometimes his grace breaks in and through us in such a way that we treat water as a gift, share with the poor, and make peace. So let us be careful to say what we mean; a saner theology that recognizes that God is unchanging, knows our needs before we speak them, and delights that we are asking for his power to change the world. To return to my earlier meteorological example, I do not think we should pray that God send rain, but I certainly think we should be on our knees morning, noon, and night praying about water.

"Dear God, in this parched land where we know how precious the gift of water really is, make us mindful of how we waste water. Help us to conserve it for the drought we have with us, or we know may not be far away. May we have enough water not only for our needs, but to share with those who have nothing to drink most of the time. We pray to the Lord."

For as Pope Benedict said in his first encyclical, "It is time to reaffirm the importance of prayer in the face of the activism and the growing secularism of many Christians engaged in charitable work. Clearly, the Christian who prays does not claim to be able to change God's plans or correct what he has foreseen. Rather, he seeks an encounter with the Father of Jesus Christ, asking God to be present with the consolation of the Spirit to him and his work" (*Deus Caritas Est* # 37).

And may the people of God say, "Amen."

CHAPTER FOUR

We are invited to respond to God's love, not forced or programmed by it.

God's will is more in the big picture than in the small.

I believe passionately in the will of God. It is just that it is discovered on the larger canvas rather than in the details. I think God is a big picture kind of guy. Let me explain.

I went through Catholic schools for all of my education. We used to pray a lot about God's will. This was especially true when vocation directors turned up to ask if we were being called to the priesthood or the religious life. At these times, some people would be praying fervently: "Please God do not call me to be a priest." "Do not make me become a nun." "Do not send me off to be a brother." The way God's call was presented to us was that first God calls you, and if you heard or felt that call, you had to respond, or else God would be very angry and you would be very unhappy because, whatever you chose to do in life, it would not be what God primarily called you to do. In Catholic circles, this sort of thinking almost exclusively applied to vocations to ordained or professed ministry within the church. Curiously, it never applied to the single or married vocation.

This idea of how a vocation works is very limited. The respondent does not seem to have much freedom in responding. They are called and that's that, whether they like it or not. I think I have met priests and religious who live out of this paradigm. They

25

did God a big favor by joining up, but they appear to have been desperately unhappy ever since. But since God called them, what else could they do? Unfortunately, they have projected their unhappiness on to countless numbers of children and adults among whom they have ministered, and the poor priests and fellow religious with whom they have lived. They really wanted to be somewhere else, doing something else, and being someone else. Having seen the havoc their vocation has wreaked, I think they should do just that.

At a very deep level, you have to want to be married to your spouse, live as a single person for life, or be a nun, brother, or priest. St. Ignatius Loyola, the founder of the Jesuits, was very keen on saying that God works in and through our desires, purified as they should be. If we do not actually desire the vocation we are discerning, then we are going to be miserable, and I cannot see how God rejoices in that fact, or how we can be satisfied that we made the best choice. Incredibly, I have met some outstanding religious and priests who say that they never wanted their vocation, and would never have chosen it, but in fact, their ministry has proved that they are excellent at it. For whatever complex reason, and paying every respect to them, I think they may be deluding themselves, and that in the depth of their being they want to be a religious or a priest. They have chosen their path.

Even in the story of the annunciation, Mary did not have to say "yes" to the angel. Notwithstanding the grace of the immaculate conception, if Mary did not have the power and freedom to say no, then her yes is insignificant. She would have been God's victim, not the model she is for us of cooperating with God, even when such a yes ended up costing her everything. Our yes to grace sometimes does the same.

In the same vein, if a bride and groom do not freely and knowingly choose each other, then the church says that their marriage is invalid. The exercise of freedom to choose and knowing what we are choosing, as much as we can, is essential to the character of marriage. What fits for this call fits for all callings in life. It may not be easy. We may struggle with it. But the reality is that we have to choose it, and in the process of discerning what we really want, what we desire, we discover God's will. If we are forced, or frightened of other alternatives, and indeed if we have no alternatives at all, then we are not making a free and knowing choice, and our response is compromised.

Therefore, on one level I do not think God cares whether I am a Jesuit or a priest. I think God wants me to live out the theological virtues of faith, hope, and love (1 Cor 13) and, for good measure, he wants each of us to embody in all that we do the fruit of the Spirit: love, joy, peace, patience, kindness, goodness, faithfulness, gentleness, and self-control (Gal 5:22). This call is not just for me, but for all God's children everywhere; that is why an inescapable dimension of our faith in God is to work for justice. We can glimpse the establishment of the reign of God in this world, as well as in the next, by creating a community where all people can realize their potential to live lives worthy of their calling to be faithful, hopeful, and loving. There is not a heavenly blueprint, as such, for my life. Through the blessing of time and place, the gifts of nature and grace, I work with God to realize my potential in the greatest way possible, even if that involves having to do things that are difficult, demanding, and sacrificial. This response is not out of fear and compulsion, but comes from love and desire.

The greatest test for the proponents of God's will as a blueprint for each individual life, and indeed for every living thing, is not found in most of our of lives, but in the lives of the poorest of the poor. Whatever my angst may be over what I might choose with God's grace to do with my life, what about a child who dies from malnutrition hours after being born? Or the twenty-eight-week-old fetus who in some countries can now be legally aborted? And the list could go on and on. Are any of these tragic situations God's active, specific will for these sisters and brothers of ours?

On a more mundane level, we sometimes hear people say after they narrowly missed being involved in an accident, "But for the grace of God, it could have been me involved in that misfortune." In other words, it was not God's will that I was involved, this time. But my problem with this is not that someone avoided being in an accident, but rather what we are saying about the poor people who were involved. It would seem we are saying that it was God's will that they be involved in the calamity. Mind you, I recall the story of the elderly Jesuit priest who was nearly run over by a car one afternoon. That night, as he was recounting his near-miss to his Jesuit community, he concluded his triumphant tale by saying without irony or insight, "But for the grace of God I would be in heaven tonight."

We can see, therefore, that the way we imagine the nature of God destines how we consider God's will. If we believe in Zeus, then we have to do things all the time to keep him on our side. Furthermore, if we see God as the divine tyrant spoken of in chapter one, then not doing the tyrant's specific will ends in grief not only in this world, but also in the next. He knows everything, even the unknowable, and so what we have to do is find out what he knows about our future and do it. This theology is operative in the story of the Jesuit priest who fell off his bicycle and broke his collar bone. The bone needed pinning, and as he was preparing for surgery, a religious sister bought him holy communion. After she gave it to him. Sister said, "Father, it is obviously God's will that you slow down and have a really good rest." To which the Jesuit replied, "If that's true, Sister, I'm pleased that God didn't think I needed a sabbatical."

Given that faith, hope, and love mark out God's will in the

big picture, and that God and I have to work out the details together, then the task of discernment comes into its own. From my reading of St. Ignatius on discernment in the *Spiritual Exercises*, his letters, and other writings, here are twelve contemporary spins on his timeless wisdom.

1. Trust the commonplace, the ordinary, the everyday. Live in the here and now. Sometimes we live in an unhealed past or an unknown future, whereas God may be found right under our nose, here and now. The good spirit draws us to deal with our ordinary life as it is, not as we may like it to be, and there discern his presence. We often look for God in the spectacular and extraordinary, and he is to be found in quiet and mundane moments, and he comes to us poor, naked, in prison, hungry, and thirsty. We need to be wary of false consolation. "The good can be the enemy of the better." We are both attacked at the most vulnerable parts of ourselves, and allured by the narcotics of modern living (drugs, alcohol, sex, work, gambling, technology, and shopping), which never take away the pain of living but temporarily mask its effects.

2. Do not make a decision when we are down; allow the crisis to pass. Sometimes we make the worst decisions when we are under pressure. It is always better to let a crisis pass and then in calmer surroundings weigh all our options.

3. Be suspicious of "the urgent." Sometimes we have to make a big decision quickly. Buying some time, any time, is always helpful for working out the best course of action. The good spirit brings a sense of perspective and priority to problems. We need to be especially careful of making a life-changing decision that goes against another life choice made properly in a time of consolation, and at peace.

29

4. Be humble enough to take wise advice wisely. We are not meant to be "rocks and islands" operating on our own. We need the wisdom of our families and most trusted friends, the church, and sometimes professionals to inform our consciences and make the best possible decisions before God. Remember that the word *obedience* comes from the Latin word *obedire*, meaning "to listen." If we all want to be obedient to God's reign in our world and lives, we had better get good at listening, in all its forms, because we believe that God listens to and hears us.

5. There are always patterns to the action of the good and bad spirit in our lives. Sometimes we think something "came out of nowhere." Sometimes it does, but most times the good and bad that beset us have a history and a context. We have to train ourselves to read the signs of both, cultivate the things that are good, and see the empty promises of the bad spirit and how it leads us into dead ends. A daily examination of conscience helps us to see the pattern of the Holy Spirit.

6. About the best summary of the good and bad spirit is from Patrick O'Sullivan, SJ, in his *Prayer and Relationships: Staying Connected, An Ignatian Perspective.* He gives the following neat descriptions of the traits of the good and bad spirits.

Signs of the Bad Spirit	Signs of the Good Spirit
Loss of the sense of our own worth. We are down on ourselves and think (and even speak) of ourselves in ways we would never dream of speaking about anyone else.	*There is a real sense of our own worth—a renewed confidence.*
Hope is blighted and fades away; the light goes out. There is a feeling of being stuck or trapped,	*Hope comes alive; we believe Jesus is with us, no matter what.* There is a genuine feeling of

of having nowhere to go, or going round in circles, of being down a big, black hole.

movement: "It hasn't got to be like this. I want to do something about it, and I can do something about it.

There is a pervasive sense of heaviness; we feel burdened. We degenerate into cynicism (we cannot see any good in anyone), or self-pity.

Something lifts from us; we feel lighter, liberated. We grow in compassion and sensitivity to the needs of others.

A questioning that creates anxiety and ends in confusion. We find ourselves mulling constantly over incidents, or giving all our attention to resolving some issue—and end up more fragmented and de-energised than when started.

A questioning that is accompanied by clarity and conviction. We are led to bring our concerns into our relationship with Jesus, and focus on the relationship rather than on the issue. We tell Him (even repeatedly!) how the issue affects us.

We are easily led into negative interactions with others that degenerate into mutual recriminations, and an "I'm right, you're wrong" attitude. "Some people carry in their hearts the corpses of past relationships, addicted to hurt as a confirmation of identity."

(It) is necessary to suppose that every good Christian is more ready to put a good interpretation on another's statement than to condemn it as false." (None of us has a monopoly on the truth.) We are led to let go of our hurts and are able to pray, "Jesus, give me the attitude [toward] this person You want me to have."

When we think of our sins and failings, we feel bad about ourselves, and stay there.

Awareness of sin is always tinged with hope and leads us back into the relationship with Jesus, and others.

Patrick O'Sullivan concludes, "The way of the bad spirit is to lead us away from relationships; the way of the good spirit is to lead us more deeply into relationships. What we give our attention to, colors all the other areas of our life. If we focus on negativity, the negativity will spread; if we focus on 'grace' (which is life-giving), the grace will spread."

Continuing the twelve contemporary spins on the wisdom of Ignatius:

7. A good or better decision is just one decision away. The bad spirit always convinces us we are trapped and there is no way out, diminishing our memory so we keep repeating destructive behavior even though it never helps; it alienates us, and does not help us deal with our situation. A journal can help wherein we review our life and its patterns with compassion and courage. For large discernments, we can draw up a list on one side of the page with the movements for A, the movements for B, the movements against A, and the movements against B. The process does not focus on which list is the longer, but where our heart and head are drawn.

8. The good spirit connects us and frees us to bring into the open anything we keep buried in the dark. The bad spirit divides, isolates, and locks us in our fears. Every time we are transparent with those we love and trust, then the good spirit is at work. There is nothing we have ever done, are doing, or will do, that will stop God from loving us. There is nothing that God cannot forgive and heal, but we have to start with owning up to who we are and what we have done. Then anything and everything is possible.

9. The Holy Spirit is always present where a community of faith in God gathers. In the community, we discover that we are not the only ones who have ever had to make a particular choice or that we are not the first to face similar problems.

10. Get our heads and hearts in dialogue—we need both. Some believers think that Christian faith is all cerebral. And while

theology has a venerable intellectual tradition, and thinking clearly is very important, our heads have to be in touch with our affective lives and our instincts. When our head and heart are more integrated, we have a good chance at putting our hands and feet in a place where we will do the greatest good for the greatest number. Our head can be filled with dreams, some of them good. Our heart and gut can hold desires. Which persist? Which ones lose their appeal over time? What are our deepest desires? These can be tested against the love, joy, peace, patience, kindness, generosity, faithfulness, and self-control we are called to live (Gal 5:22). If these signs are present, then chances are, so is the Holy Spirit.

11. No work for the coming of the kingdom is too small, irrelevant, or inconsequential. We can often be conned into thinking that our relatively small and daily acts of kindness do not count for much in the spiritual scheme of things. Wrong. If there were more evil actions than loving actions in our world on any one day, the earth would be personally unlivable. Simple and selfless acts of kindness might go unreported, but they change the world by enabling Christ's love to break through into the world of our daily lives.

12. Fidelity is one of the greatest gifts of the Spirit. Even in the face of opposition and other choices, remaining faithful is a heroic act of love. That said, the Gospel calls us to "die unto self," not to "kill self." It is never God's will, for example, for a person to stay in a physically, emotionally, and spiritually violent relationship. Ignatius encourages us to imagine we are advising our best friend about the matter we have under discernment. What would your counsel be? Alternatively, imagine being on our deathbed. What choices do we wish we had

made as we reviewed our life? Hopefully, they would be the most loving, faithful, and hopeful ones.

Discerning from a position of being in love is superbly sum-marized in one of my favorite quotes attributed to the former supe-rior general of the Jesuits, Pedro Arrupe, SJ:

> "Nothing is more practical than finding God, that is, than falling in love in a quite absolute, final way. What you are in love with, what seizes your imagination, will affect every-thing. It will decide what will get you out of bed in the morning, what you do with your evenings, how you spend your weekends, what you read, who you know, what breaks your heart, and what amazes you with joy and gratitude. Fall in love, stay in love, and it will decide everything."

CHAPTER FIVE

*If God did that to his only beloved Son,
maybe I'm getting off lightly.*

God did not *need* the blood of Jesus. Jesus did not just come "to die,"
but God used his death to announce the end to death.

It amazes me how some Christians can believe so strongly and tell
others so forcefully that God sends them pain, destruction, and
death when there is so much evidence that we believe in a God
who wants nothing to do with death and its courtiers. God wants
life, liberty, and joy for us.

We should be very careful about what we sing. Spiritual
songs and hymns are not part of our liturgy to fill in time, accompany a procession, or annoy the tone deaf who are pressed into
making a noise. Hymns carry theology. We sing scriptural texts or
a poetic version of a fundamental Christian truth to affirm our
faith. Setting these texts to music makes them popular and memo-
rable. That is why they can be so powerful and important, but also
dangerous.

Take for example the spiritual song "The Man God Chose"
that was popular for a while. The man in question is Jesus. It was a
very singable and likable folk melody, and many of the sentiments
within it were worthy. The problem with this hymn is that the sincere songwriter did not know that he was giving a modern plat-
form to an ancient heresy, and that now congregations were

standing and singing it with gusto. This hymn is a modern take on some of the writings of Paul of Samosata and Theodotus of Byzantium, who held that Jesus was adopted or chosen by God at his baptism and, because of the exemplary human life he then led, was confirmed as the Son at the crucifixion. This position was condemned in the late third century. God did not choose or adopt Jesus. We believe that the Word and Wisdom of God took flesh in Jesus of Nazareth from the moment of his conception.

Hymns matter, and one verse of one hymn has more to answer for than most. "How Great Thou Art" takes its place in the top five of nearly every survey of the most loved hymns in the English speaking world. Written by the Swedish Lutheran lay preacher and later parliamentarian Carl Gustav Boberg in 1885, "O Store Gud" (O Great God) was translated into English by Stuart Hine. Hine was an English evangelical missionary in Ukraine, where he learned the hymn in Russian. In 1939, he returned to England and the following year published the first version of the hymn we now call "How Great Thou Art." Its worldwide fame can be attributed to Billy Graham's international crusade in London in 1954, during which time this hymn was sung over and over as it accompanied the altar call, and was broadcast and televised to an audience of millions. It did not hurt the hymn's fortunes that it was the Grammy Award-winning title song of Elvis Presley's 1967 hit record.

The Protestant pedigree of this hymn is important. A little history first. Building on the earlier work of St. Clement of Alexandria, St. Anselm of Canterbury, an 11th-century Benedictine monk, wrestled with the question why God came into the world as one like us. In his famous treatise, *Cur Deus Homo* (Why God Became Human), he developed a theory that Jesus came into the world to act as a substitute for us. We were the ones who had offended God, but rather than sacrifice us all, God sent Jesus to take our place in offering up his own life to the Father as restitution for our sins. He paid the ransom that God demanded to set us free.

This way of thinking relies heavily upon St. Paul, where on many occasions he calls Christ our Redeemer. The word *redemption* literally means, "buying back." It comes from the practice in the ancient world where there were two types of slaves—those who were born or forced into slavery, usually for life, and those who paid off a debt or a crime by becoming a slave, usually for a period of time. The second type of slave could be set free when someone else paid their debts, or the ransom their master now demanded for them was settled. They would then either be the slave of the pur- chaser, or set free completely.

St. Paul introduced this metaphor into Christian theology to describe how we, who are enslaved by our destructive behavior, gained a liberator in Christ who entered into a sinful world, sub- jected himself to its violence and death, in order to set us free. At its best, the notion of Christ the Redeemer shows us that we do not have to live destructively anymore. Now claimed by the love of Christ, we are no longer slaves, but his friends; indeed, through the redeeming work of Christ we have been welcomed into God's family.

The Protestant Reformers took up these substitution ideas and gave them a more biblical spin. Relying on a literal and tougher stand on the role of the Fall of Adam and Eve, John Calvin held that, because the first parents of humanity in the Book of Genesis rebelled against God, our whole human nature was corrupted for- ever. There was nothing we could do about it. God was so angry with us that, in time and in his mercy, and even though we did not deserve it, he decided to save us. However, because humanity could not do anything to save itself, to satisfy God's wrath at

Adam and Eve and all humanity's subsequent ingratitude, the Word of God had to take our flesh, our place, and offer up the sacrifice of his own life in and through his suffering and death as atonement for our inherited and ongoing sinfulness. It is often called "satisfaction theology" because it was through the violent death of Jesus that God's wrath was satisfied. It must be admitted that some elements of this satisfaction theology continue in Catholic theology as well, though we have never held that humanity was totally corrupt or depraved, and that God had only one option in appeasing his own anger.

There are libraries written on the stuff of the last couple of paragraphs, but for our purposes here, this wholly inadequate summary will have to do.

In its more stark form, satisfaction theology is given a full confessional expression in the third verse of "How Great Thou Art":

When I think that God his Son not sparing
Sent him to die, I scarce can take it in.
That on the Cross my burden gladly bearing,
He bled and died to take away my sin.

Why does this matter? Well, if we keep singing hymns like this, then some people may think it is true, may remember it, and want it sung at all their family's baptisms, weddings, funerals, and other rites of passage. And they do. But this hymn gives a very limited version of the truth it is trying to articulate, and the implications it holds in regard to where God is to be found in our suffering and pain cannot be underestimated. God's will for Jesus affects everything about how we think God deals with us. If our God wants and sends suffering, even setting up a grizzly death for his only beloved son, then why should we complain when we get a disease, an illness, lose a child, or become a quadriplegic? We are getting off lightly in comparison to what some claim God wanted from Jesus.

For Christians, the paschal mystery—the life, death, and resurrection of Jesus—is the central paradigm around which our faith in God is constructed. It is the central story through which we explain our own origins, meaning, and destiny. This hymn concerns itself with this mystery, and I can scarcely take in that God simply sent Jesus "to die," and to die a gruesome and bloody death, at that. If that were baldly true, then why did God spare him from the outcome of the most unjust theological story in the New Testament—the slaughter of the innocents (Matt 2:13—23)? If Jesus was murdered by Herod at two years of age, then God could have gotten his blood sacrifice over nice and early.

Alternatively, if all God wanted was the perfect blood offering (echoes of Zeus here) of his only Son for the sake of appeasing his anger, why did Jesus not leave Nazareth, stir up plenty of trouble around Galilee (as he did), and then march straight into Jerusalem and offend everyone and get crucified early on? It would not have been hard. If Jesus was simply sent "to die," then what was the point of his hidden years and the public ministry? They were not there for God's sake, but for ours.

The simple truth is that the third verse of this beloved hymn is wrong. Jesus did not simply come to die. Rather, Jesus came to live. As a result of the courageous and radical way he lived his life, and the saving love he embodied for all humanity, he threatened the political, social, and religious authorities of his day so much that they executed him. This is, I think, an easier way for us to make sense of the predictions of the passion. Jesus was not clairvoyant; he was a full and true human being and therefore had informed but limited knowledge. His full and true divinity cannot

WHERE THE HELL IS GOD?

obliterate his humanity or else he would be play-acting at being human. His divinity is seen in and through the uncompromisingly loving, just, and sacrificial way he lived within the bounds of his humanity.

Many of the most morally courageous people in history knew that their personal life and liberty were threatened because of what they were saying or how they were living. They may not have known beforehand *that* they would be executed or murdered or assassinated, but they could read the signs of their times well enough to predict that there were serious consequences to the freedom they were embodying and to which they were attracting other people. Sometimes they spoke or wrote about the cost of the stands they took. In this regard, they reflect Jesus Christ. Our martyrs are not Christian versions of suicide bombers. They do not go looking for death in any active sense. That would be the ultimate betrayal of God's gift of life. They know, however, *that* they may die as a result of witnessing to their faith and the demand for justice that must flow from it. In their lives and deaths they follow the pattern of Jesus. He did not seek death for its own sake, but would not and could not live any other way than faithfully, hopefully, and lovingly. In his day, as in our own, this is immensely threatening to those whose power base is built on values opposed to these virtues. The world continues to silence and sideline people who live out the Christian virtues and values now, just as Jesus was thought to be ultimately sidelined in his crucifixion. But God had the last word on the death of Jesus: Life.

For most of Christian history, the question that has vexed many believers seems to be, "Why did Jesus die?" I think it is the wrong question. The right one is "Why was Jesus killed?" And that puts the last days of Jesus' suffering and death in an entirely new perspective.

This is how we can stand before the cross and listen to Jesus in John's Gospel say, "I have come that you may have life, and have it to the full." This life is not about the perfect Son of the perfect Father making the perfect sacrifice to get us back in God's good books, and thereby saving us. It is the Trinity's inner life overflowing to the world in Christ through the power of the Spirit.

Our God does not deal in death, but life. Everything in the New Testament shows this, even the grand apocalyptic narratives about the end of time, which show all the hallmarks of an inspired rabbinic teacher drawing big strokes on the largest of canvases. Jesus did not intend us to take this imagery literally. I assume the experience of judgment will not actually be a livestock muster of sheep and goats. However, the lesson behind the imagery is a real one for us to learn. God's compassion and love will ultimately see that justice is done. He will hear the cry of the poor and we will be called to account in the next life for what we have done and what we have failed to do in this life.

In this context we need to look at one other gospel text. Some people quote Jesus in the garden saying, "My Father, if this cup cannot pass unless I drink it, thy will be done" (Matt 26:42) or "Put your sword back into its sheath. Am I not to drink the cup that the Father has given me?" (John 18:11) as conclusive proof that God wanted and even needed Jesus to suffer and die. It all depends on what we think the will or the cup of the Father is for Jesus. If it is, as the hymn sings, "to die," then that is quite clear and final. However, if, as argued earlier, the will of God is that we are faithful, hopeful, and loving, then Jesus' prayer is about the Father strengthening and emboldening the Son to stay on the Way, to speak and be the Truth, and to witness to the Life, even if it costs him his own. Such a life of transparent goodness is never easy; it always involves a cup of suffering. In the garden scene we have

Jesus becoming aware of his impending doom and struggling to finally claim the power to confront death and destruction and sin head-on. Jesus' anguish at whatever might be his fate is an entirely human response, one that consoles all of us as we face our own anxieties.

God the Father's role in the context of accompanying his Son in and through the crucible of anxiety in the garden might be seen in terms of a just and good army commander. A good friend of mine who has led troops into battle in Afghanistan says, "I love my troops so much that I would never want to commit them to death. I have gone with them into battle only so that we can all serve the higher good of liberating people from tyranny and offering them a better life than anything they've known before. The time before any known battle is the most anxious of times when any man or woman worth his or her salt is filled with self-doubt and wishes they were anywhere but there. But the higher calling is to remain focused on the mission, and be committed to the people, among the poorest people in the world, to whom we are sent to serve. Believing in the rightness of the cause means we can overcome our worst anxieties, look death in the face, and make sure evil does not have the last word. The worst moments of my life, so far, have been to return to base having lost any of my troops. I can be inconsolable for a while, only comforted by knowing that they were as committed to the mission as I was and believing that their death was not in vain, but in helping make the world a better place." In this context, Jesus' cup of suffering is not imposed by God from without but is the consequence of liberating us from tyranny, offering us the fullness of life in this world and the next, and making sure that evil did not have, and does not have, the last word.

And think about what we have done to the cross of Christ. Many of us now wear small crosses and crucifixes in rolled gold, platinum, or sterling silver. They dangle around our necks or from our earlobes. I wonder, if the Romans had access to the electric chair rather than the cross, whether we would now have small silver, gold, or platinum electric chairs around our necks and hanging from our earlobe. Furthermore, rather than starting our prayers with the sign of the cross, we might assume the grip of one in an electric chair and begin our prayers with, "Szszszsz." This provocative and contemporary image brings home what Paul calls the scandal or "foolishness" of the cross (1 Cor 1:18—26). The cross of Christ is not a fashion accessory, no matter how many of them Madonna and Eminem wear. Looking upon it should still take our breath away, not only because it shows us how far Jesus was prepared to go in establishing his reign of justice and love in this world, but also because it spells out the cost for all of us who follow his Way, speak his Truth, and live his Life. This should be as radical and threatening now as it was in the first century. For those of us who put on a cross, and for everyone who carries one, we want to answer Christ's question, "How far will you go out of love in following me?" with the same answer he gave the Father, and us, "I will go to the end. I will see it through, no matter the cost."

Sometimes when we ask, "Where the hell is God?" some Christians will avoid the answer to that question and simply tell us to "offer it up." By this they mean to say, "Well, God required Jesus to suffer a torturous death, so you must see in your own suffering and pain God offering you the same cup of suffering as he offered Jesus." It is not that long ago that these ideas had such currency that we "offered up" our suffering for the salvation of souls in purgatory, or for others whose lives we thought offended God. My concern is not that Jesus suffered and died and that so do we, but what sort of image of God emerges from understanding our salvation in terms of the commercial transaction of paying a ransom, or an angry God deriving satisfaction from us "offering up" our suffering, illness, and pain, which he has sent to us in the first place.

Another traditional way of understanding our suffering is to say that in "offering it up," we are freely uniting our sufferings with the sufferings of Jesus, so they then take on some meaning. If my thoughts on why Jesus suffered hold true, then we could reclaim that approach but with an important difference. Rather than the implied belief that it is about the further appeasement of a needy God—a view that is difficult given that Jesus' sacrifice was once and for all—I find meaning in my suffering by being faithful to Jesus' Way, Truth, and Life, when every other instinct in me wants to cut and run. Here we find God in my Gethsemane enabling me to confront death and destruction and sin head-on, now confident through the experience of Jesus that the life of God will have the last word.

I like creative and stirring arrangements of "How Great Thou Art." I am very happy to sing strongly about how we can wander through the woods and glades and praise "all the worlds Thy Hands have made." And in the final verse, I sing more loudly than anyone about "When Christ shall come, with shout of acclamation and take me home what joy shall fill my soul." It is just verse three. Because I take popular theology seriously, I cannot and will not sing it because I hope the verse, and the bloodthirsty God behind it, just isn't true. In fact, what makes God great is that he wants nothing to do with death.

CHAPTER SIX

"Thus have we made the world."

God has created a world that is less than perfect, or else it would be heaven, and in which suffering, disease, and pain are realities. Some of these we now create for ourselves and blame God.

The title to this chapter comes from Robert Bolt's masterful screenplay for the film *The Mission*. The very last line of dialogue in the film belongs to the papal envoy Cardinal Altamirano. Having given permission for the invading Portuguese and Spanish to forcefully invade the Jesuit missions above the falls and enslave many of the Guarani, he now sees the extent of the destruction that flowed from his freely chosen decision. Señor Hontar consoles the cardinal, "We must work in the world, Your Eminence. The world is thus." To which Altamirano replies, "No, Señor Hontar. Thus have we made the world...thus have I made it."

It was noted earlier that philosophers and theologians regularly make a distinction between different types of evil: moral, physical, and metaphysical. These distinctions rightly matter in academic circles, but they count for less to the person in the street. Evil exists, and God has at least permitted it. There has always been overlap between these categories, and never as much as now. With the help of science and the media, we are seeing the extent of the impact of our lives on one another and the created world. There are still some people, often atheists, who say, "You all believe in a

45

God of love, and yet there are famines and wars. I will believe in your God when these things stop." I will soon return to the fact that God has to take some responsibility for the world as it is, but for now I want to deal with the overlap between moral and physical evil. Starvation is the most confronting example.

Every time there is another famine in the world, someone says, "How could God let that happen?" Sometimes we may think like this too. The statistics on starvation are frightening. We have enough food in our world to feed the estimated 6.7 billion people who live on this planet. So food production is not the issue. The issue has much more to do with the distribution of food, the means of production, and the social and political climate of the places where most of the world lives. The United Nations says that 5.5 billion people live in what the World Bank considers "developing countries," that is, about 82 percent of the human family. The World Bank says that at least 80 percent of humanity lives on U.S.$10 a day or less, and that the G-20, the twenty richest countries in the world, possesses three-quarters of the world's wealth.

It is impossible to have absolutely reliable figures, but in a world where we could feed everyone, UNICEF estimates that 16 thousand children die each day from starvation. That means 11 children die every minute of every day. And this does not include the adults. In this context, we can see how moral evil moves over to physical evil, and not just in the sense of weather. Most famines are no longer caused solely by droughts or floods. The Food and Agriculture Organization says that general poverty, lack of democracy, civil war, and unjust access to world markets are as much to blame for starvation as climatic factors, if not more so now. Therefore, when people say, "Why does God let famine and starvation happen," I imagine God shaking his head in a tearful reply, "Why do you let famine and starvation happen?" In most of the wealthy countries of the world, elections are fought on economics, but the people who have the least rarely rate a mention. Can any of us recall a candidate who was or was not elected because of his or her stand on third world development? When did we last hear a significant stump speech or a campaign debate about what any of the political parties are going to do for the 80 percent of the world's population who will not vote in our elections, but whose life and death may be in part destined by it? When did we ask our elected officials for their policy in regard to intervening to stop general poverty, lack of democracy, civil war, and unjust access to world markets for all God's children?

God becomes a convenient whipping boy at this point, but the ball is squarely in our court. In a world where all people could be fed, why do people starve? We choose it to be this way. Indeed, some frustrated economists who work in this area go as far as to say the G20 needs it this way and structures the global market accordingly. Regardless of the details, the evil here is ours, and God will call us to account for it. And because of access to the many forms of media, we will not be able to say to God that we did not know either the scale of the problem or our complicity within it. Ignorance cannot be our defense. The same is true of other examples as well: environmental degradation, personal and social stress, and lack of action to end war. We choose the world to be like this, and then blame God for the negative fallout from our decisions.

Of course, in our Christian tradition, we have regular reminders of our obligations to God's poor, our sisters and brothers, and giving to charity. I know that in many Christian families, institutions, and even among religious and clergy, saying grace before meals is dying out. I think this is a pity. I am often invited to people's homes for dinner, and as the cook calls the adults to the table, the young people have already arrived and are already eating by the time we get there. At this sight, the mother or father will say, "Hang on a minute, kids, Father is going to say grace." The 16-year-old looks up and says, "Why are we saying grace? We never say grace. Why are we putting on a show for the priest?" I never mind a bit that my presence reminds others of what I think we should do at every meal: say thank you for this food and ask that the strength this meal gives us enables us to make the world a more just place for all people everywhere. It is a thrice-daily reminder that we are creating the world as it is.

The second tradition we have is to give money to charity, especially Christian charities that are motivated in their work to eliminate the burden of poverty by the same values that motivate our lives too. The best of Christian charities, like Caritas, spend the least on administration costs and empower local people to make the best and most transparent decisions about where and how the money should be spent. Christian development and charity are not optional extras in our lives. This commitment recognizes that our obligation to be generous increases with the blessings that we receive.

Nevertheless, it remains true that God must take some responsibility for the world in which we live. He permits evil things to take place. As noted earlier, I am not given much to speculation about whether this is the best possible world or not. It is the world we have, and I accept it as the place wherein we exercise our free will to make it the best one we can have. By virtue of our choices, we can improve upon it, or leave it impoverished. But here I want to make one point. Some people speak about the world in such terms that lead me to conclude that they want it to be perfect. In Christian theology, at least, this would mean it would be heaven, so we have to accept that anything less than heaven allows for the possibility of a world that is less than perfect. In this less than perfect place, then, we exercise our free will that, as we know from personal and social experience, can be a mixed blessing in what it bestows on us, others, and the world. Free will is such a critical gift for humanity that to give it with one hand and then create a perfect world within which to exercise it, would mean we would never see the fruit of our good choices, or the destructiveness of our poor ones. And this leads me to God's power, or more precisely, how God might exercise that power in the world.

Now, traditional theology holds that God is one, does not change, is not caused by any other being, is transcendent, all-powerful, all-knowing, all-present, and is holy or all-loving. I accept all these things, but the last two I want to cling to for dear life in any discussion about evil.

If God goes to sleep or takes vacations from the world, as some Jewish theologians argue must have happened from 1939—1945, then we are really in trouble. It means the world goes into free fall for a while, and could explain how on October 23, 1998, God dozed off at the wheel of the world, while my sister was alert at the wheel of her car. I cannot imagine that to be true. God looks lazy or negligent. I need to hold on to the fact that God is always present to us as a companion in the vicissitudes of life and death. This is what the Christian doctrine of the incarnation is about. God so wanted to attend us, and so that we might be loved and saved from evil and ourselves, he became one with us in our flesh. Christianity is the only world religion to assert this extraordinary truth.

The second element within the nature of God that I think we need to underline in this discussion is God's holiness and love. We explored this in chapter one, but the God of Jesus Christ does not have an ugly, vengeful, and dark side. "God is love," St. John tells us. Love defines God's nature, was expressed in human form in

Jesus, and is active in the ongoing action of the Spirit who inspires movements, choices, and works of love in us.

Therefore, the one God who, as we have seen earlier, must be unchanging, otherwise we would never know where we stand, is not created by any other power or being, and is transcendent. This leads us to God's power and knowledge. I have no problem accepting that God is, in himself, all-powerful and all-knowing. Indeed, I need God to be precisely that. There is no point having a God who has deficiencies in these regards. If it were otherwise, I think I would want to trade in this God for another, later and better, model. The issue is not about God's ability to know and do, but how God's power and knowledge are exercised in regard to the world, in regard to us, and in this regard I find myself moving away from traditional arguments about God's knowledge or omniscience and his power.

There are two ways I have found helpful to understand what God might know and can do. The first is to accept that God does not know the unknowable and cannot do the undoable. If something is beyond knowing or beyond doing, is that true for God as well as for us? In popular discussion, people will quickly reply to this thesis, "But God is God. He knows everything and can do anything." If this is true, then the unknowable is knowable, at least to God, and he chooses not to share it even with those who seemingly most need to know it, and the undoable is doable at least to God, who decides not to act, even though his inaction has such destructive results for the very people who believe in his presence and love. Alternatively, there are things God does not know and cannot do because God chooses it that way. I concede that this is a departure from traditional Christian doctrine of what God is like in his essence. But it seems to me that the expression of traditional theology has to trade away some of God's care and love, and maybe even God's presence, to hold on to God's power and knowledge, so let me give you a human example of how my idea might work.

At the risk of anthropomorphizing God, that is, making God in our image and likeness, my example is that of a parent of a teenager. A loving mother or father of a 17-year-old may well want to shield their daughter or son from the potential pain and grief of the world by knowing everything that is happening in their child's life and by constantly intervening at the first hint of trouble. As loving and present as these parents might seem, chances are, their son or daughter will be immature as they progress through their late adolescence, unprepared for adulthood by their well-intentioned but suffocating and controlling parents. They will have stunted growth. The reality is that, at least in Western society, there comes a point in a loving relationship between parents and teenage children when parents have to let their children make their own decisions, not know everything there is to know, and stop intervening at the first sign of trouble. It can be frustrating and even heartbreaking for parents, but the decision to limit parental knowledge and power does not come out of malice, or because they do not care, but precisely the opposite—because they care enough to accept that young adults need to know they are supported and have their parents' companionship as they explore their own world.

If this holds true for the best of loving parents in this world, why cannot it be true of our relationship with God? It has long been accepted in philosophy that God treats us like adults, that we are not God's marionettes, his playthings. Therefore, in dealing with us, and in supporting us to achieve our full potential, God could know everything, but chooses not to, and could keep intervening, but chooses not to. These self-imposed limits on knowledge and power do not occur out of malice, but out of love for us and God's desire to see us grow.

If this is true of the metaphysical world, can they also apply to God's relationship to the physical world as well?

Some time ago, the Pontifical Academy of Science in Rome invited the British theoretical physicist Stephen Hawking to address its annual meeting at the Vatican. Because Professor Hawking's area is cosmology and quantum gravity, he is a man who has thought longer than most about the ordering of the universe. He is, by his own concession, not a classical Christian believer. In an interview with Reuters, Hawking said he is "not religious in the normal sense...I believe the universe is governed by the laws of science. The laws may have been decreed by God, but God does not intervene to break the laws." When the text of this interview was published around the time of his visit to the Vatican, one blogger expressed a widely held opinion in reply to Hawking's views: "If he (God) has the power to make 'em, surely he equally has the power to break 'em. That is, he transcends them." Well, in a sense, I imagine you could argue he could, but why would God set up physical laws only to keep breaking them all the time? It could mean God is making it up as he goes along, but this hardly instills much confidence in us toward God. We become an elaborate experiment. Traditional theology holds God can do anything that is not against his nature, like committing sin, and does not involve contradiction (like making a rock that God could not lift). Allied to this is that, if God can make 'em and break 'em, then, in a sense, I wish he would do much more of it, and intervene to stop all sorts of innocent people from suffering from physical evil. The blogger here is quick to defend God's power, but at the expense of God's unchangeability and love.

Regardless of what God can do, Hawking's position is a reasonable one in the face of the predictable physical structures of the universe we have been able to grasp so far. To keep the blogger happy, however, we could say that God could break 'em, but chooses not to. This divine restraint, of course, is another departure from traditional theology but need not be a sign of weakness within God, but a revelation of stunning strength. God does not need to show off. He does not need our approval. And it would seem that such is his power—and maybe his solidarity with us— that he accompanies us in this finite journey with a mature love for us, choosing not to know and not to keep intervening. So what then of miracles?

That miracles occur seems to be beyond dispute, especially in the realm of physical, emotional, or spiritual healing. In Christian dogma, the believer is required to affirm that miracles happen, and that the author of the miracle is God. Like many fellow Christian travelers whom I know, I also share a healthy interest and belief in miracles. I do not, however, believe that they come from without. I believe God works miracles from within. I have no concept of God "zapping" people with miraculous power. Such an idea can reduce God to a magician, gaining the admiration of the spellbound audience who longs to see his next amazing trick. One of the many problems with this model is that the most deserving people I know, like my sister, never seem to be called up on the celestial stage. I also reject this "magic model" because I cannot find it in the actions of Jesus. "Sign faith" in John's Gospel was considered the weakest faith of all. If miracles were simply a question of God's power, then how come Jesus could not perform miracles always and everywhere? The gospel writers often put it down to a "lack of faith," which already allows for other preconditions for a miracle to occur.

Contemporary neuroscience is just starting to understand the general properties of the brain, and this organ's potential to heal. I think miracles occur when some of these healing assets are released by the brain into the body. For some, the reception of the anointing of the sick and the laying on of hands unlocks these properties. For others, it may be a pilgrimage to a holy place, personal prayer or intercessory prayer, devotion to a saint, or for other more secular people I know who have experienced a miracle, it was a complete change in lifestyle, diet, and the practice of meditation. This goes some way to explaining why Jesus could perform some miracles and not others and why, at Bethsaida, Jesus had to have a second go at healing the man born blind. Even an encounter with Jesus or a single touch was not enough for some people, while for others their master's or friend's desires to see them well were enough to effect the change. Given that Christians readily concede that the evolution of the human brain is among God's greatest handiwork, then God is, in every sense, the author of the miraculous. It is just a question of where God's grace resides. It is not just from without. Brian Doyle, in his "Grace Notes" in *Leaping: Revelations and Epiphanies*, captures the same sense: "We think of grace arriving like an ambulance, a just-in-time delivery, an invisible divine cavalry cresting a hill of troubles, a bolt of jazz from the glittering horn of the creator, but maybe it lives in us and is activated by illness of the spirit. Maybe we're loaded with grace. Maybe we're stuffed with the stuff."

Miracles happen, but I think the writers of the film *Bruce Almighty* were inspired when they placed these words on the lips of God: "Parting your soup is not a miracle, Bruce, it's a magic trick. A single mom who's working two jobs, and still finds time to take her son to soccer practice, that's a miracle. A teenager who says 'no' to drugs and 'yes' to an education, that's a miracle. People want me to do everything for them. What they don't realize is *they* have the power. You want to see a miracle, son? Be the miracle."

In this regard, as in most things, it all depends on how we read the signs. Take for example the apocryphal story about the time, many centuries ago, when the pope decided that all the Jews had to leave Rome. Rightly, there was uproar from the Jewish community. So the pope made a deal. He would have a religious debate with a member of the Jewish community. If the Jews won, they could stay. If the pope won, the Jews had to leave. The Jews realized that they had no choice. The problem was that no one wanted to debate the pope. The only volunteer was a poor, simple old man named Moishe who opened the door to the synagogue each Friday night. Not being used to words, Moishe asked for only one addition to the debate—that neither side would be allowed to talk. The pope agreed.

The day of the great debate came. Moishe and the pope sat opposite each other. The pope raised his hand and showed three fingers. Moishe looked back at him and raised one finger. The pope waved his hand in a circle around his head. Moishe pointed to the ground where he sat. The pope pulled out a wafer and a glass of wine. Moishe pulled out an apple.

The pope stood up and said, "I give up. This man is too good. The Jews can stay."

Later, the pope explained what happened: "I held up three fingers to represent the Trinity. He responded by holding up one finger to remind me that we believe in the same one God. Then I waved my hand around my head to show that God was all around us. He responded by pointing to the ground, showing that God was present right here. I pulled out the bread and wine to show that God has given us the Eucharist. He pulled out an apple to remind me of original sin. He had an answer for everything. What could I do?"

Meanwhile, Moishe explained to the Jewish scholars how he won the unwinnable debate. "Well," said Moishe, "First he said that the Jews had three days to get out of Rome. I told him that not one of us was leaving. Then he told me that this whole city would

be cleared of Jews. I let him know that we were staying right here."
"And then what clinched the debate?" asked the rabbi. "I don't
know," said Moishe. "This was the strangest thing of all: he took
out his lunch, and I took out mine!"

The challenge, then, is to read the signs of the times in our
imperfect world in such a way that apportions responsibility
where it belongs. There is plenty of it to go around. God is responsible for allowing a world to evolve within which the effects of
moral and physical evil can create injustices. But God is not
responsible because we refuse to make the hard choices that would
see our world transformed into a more just and equal place for
everyone. We will not act as one family under God. In the face of
this obstinacy, it is not surprising that we find a divine scapegoat to
carry the guilt for our lack of political will and social solidarity.
"Thus have we made the world...thus have I made it."

CHAPTER SEVEN

*When your time is up, your time is up,
and you don't get a second more.*

God does not kill us off.

I must have the word *pagan* x-rayed into my forehead because every time I go near a shopping center and I am minding my own business, I am accosted by our Christian fundamentalist brothers and sisters. Almost invariably they come up to me and ask,

"Brother, have you given your life to Jesus Christ as your personal Lord and Savior?"

"Well as a matter of fact I have."

"Do you speak in tongues?"

"I can, but I choose not to."

"Do you know the demands of living the life of the Lord?"

"Listen, mate, I think poverty, chastity, and obedience for Christ for life is a decent push in the right direction."

Although, in saying this, I think of my Jesuit vow day when a good friend, while surveying the venue for the occasion, the magnificent Jesuit real estate that is St. Ignatius College, Sydney, said to me, "Well if this is poverty, I want to see chastity."

Back to the shopping center where I am now warming up to a discussion.

"Do you mind if I ask you a couple of questions?"

"Sure."

"Do you believe the Bible is literally true in every detail?"

"Amen to that," is the stock reply.

"Well, then, maybe you can help. Was the world made in seven days or in one event—the first two chapters of Genesis have two versions. Did the angel come to Mary or Joseph? Did Jesus go to Jerusalem once or several times? Was the sermon on the mount or on the plain? Are there four Beatitudes or eight? Are there ten injunctions in the Lord's Prayer, or are there five? What were the last words of Jesus—in four Gospels we have three versions? On Easter morning, did Jesus appear first to Peter or Mary Magdalene? And when did the ascension and Pentecost happen—on Easter Sunday or forty days later?"

By this stage, a supervisor has normally approached us and suggests that, "you should move on because we do not ask questions of the Word of God, we just live it." And there, in a nutshell, is one of the problems.

As Catholics, thank God, at least since the 1960s, we do not officially take the scriptures literally. We are not biblically fundamentalist. That is, until we seem to go near texts about God knowing the "hairs on our head" and the "span of our days" (Jer 1:5; Gal 1:15—16; Prov 16:33; Matt 10:30). Then we become completely fundamentalist. In their pristine form, these verses were biblically dramatic examples of God's personal care. Not now. These texts are used to support the idea that God knows and destines the years, months, weeks, days, hours, and seconds of each life.

When I go near a nursing home, I am regularly asked, "Father, why won't God take Grandma?" To which I want to reply, "Because Grandma won't stop breathing yet." Using the cricket or baseball metaphor, we can say, "Well, Gran has had good innings." This works well enough when the person who has died is at an advanced age. The same line and its grateful sense break down completely when I am with parents who have just lost a child at any age, but especially at a stillbirth or when a child dies during its infancy. No parent should ever have to bury their child.

The rawest grief I ever see is when a child is seriously ill, or after he or she has died. Then, the parents will ask with great passion, "Where the hell is God?" And saying: "It's all a mystery," or "My ways are not your ways," or "God must have needed another angel in heaven" is not cutting the mustard. I doubt it ever did. I know well-educated parents who have walked away from the practice of their faith because no one was able to help them think through a more coherent meaning to the life and death of their children, other than to say, "We will find out in heaven, when God will wipe away all our tears." While we believe this is true, and that there is a mysterious dimension to all suffering, saying that death is a mystery does not let us off the hook from using our intelligence and reason to speculate upon some better answers. And while some of these responses may not answer all the questions we have, they might be more comforting than the banalities that pass for words of Christian comfort right now.

For the record, God does NOT need angels in heaven. In theology we say that God is sufficient. God does not need anything, and therefore he has no need to take our children from us, angelic or otherwise. What is exciting about the Christian faith is that we believe God wants us. That is why humanity was created. It is possible, I suppose, to argue that God wants some human beings so much that God takes them back to heaven quickly, prematurely, by our standards. Many sincere Christians believe this, but it is a very hard line to run in the face of a parent's loss. The tyrannical God returns, whose desires can ruin our lives. I have no problem about the journey motif common in so much of our funeral language these days, but I steer well away from talking about God "taking us," or "calling us" in and through death. I think it is unhelpful in the way it can compromise God's love and goodness. Why would God's desire "to take" a two-year-old to heaven be more than God's desire "to leave" this child in the arms of loving parents? And if God is into taking and calling the children we love in death, then why not include those who are physically and sexually abused from the youngest ages by their evil parents and families, or who are orphans standing up in their cribs with outstretched arms with no one to cuddle, love, or adopt them?

In contrast, I think it is entirely appropriate to believe that life—from the womb to the nursing home—is not allotted a span, as such, by God, but that our body will live until it can no longer function, for whatever natural or accidental reason. God is not an active player in this process, but again, has to take responsibility for making us mortal. In classical theology, the other alternative would have been for us to have been created a disembodied spirit, or an angel. But then I would not be me.

Consequently, when our body dies, our soul or spirit begins its final journey home. It is worth pausing here to reflect on what part of us might make this journey, what survives us through death. Clearly, if we cannot be certain about where God fits into a sometimes evil world, then the nature of the soul is also the stuff of speculation.

However, it is interesting that, while the spiritual conception of a soul and its use in our religious language has waned, the word *soul* persists in ordinary conversation. Many nonreligious people use this most religious of terms to describe another person. We often hear how others are lonely, distressed, or lost souls. It can be said that someone has a "beautiful soul" or that a piece of music, a painting, or other work of art "stirred my soul." We describe mellow jazz as "soulful" and still alert others to distress by an SOS, "save our souls." These uses of the word reinforce St. Thomas Aquinas' teaching that the soul makes us human and sets us apart from other animals. Nearly all the great religions of the world believe in a soul or its equivalent—something that survives the annihilation of the body in death.

I have come to the opinion that, whatever else might characterize the soul, memory is an integral part of it. Our memories survive us.

I have done several funerals of people who have suffered from Alzheimer's disease. These are rarely very sad occasions because the family invariably says that they "lost" the one they loved months or years before. Why? It is because gradually their loved one could not remember anyone or anything. We hold to caring for the body from the womb to the tomb because we believe that human dignity must always be respected. There are now theories about how even memories of the circumstances of our conception and birth may have a bearing on the way we live our lives. It is also apparent that even when people seem to have lost their memory, or are unconscious, there is some recognition of some things at a very deep level. I am struck, for example, how people who suffer from Alzheimer's disease and cannot remember who they are or where they are, can still construct perfect sentences in their native language, and sometimes in other languages they have learned in their lifetime. Language is a profound exercise in memory, even when the meaning of the stated sentences can be quite confused.

Memory, as a constitutive element within my soul, means that when I meet God face to face, I will remember who I am and how I lived, and God will remember me. It is also a comfort for us to think that we may be reunited with those we have loved and who have died before us, because we remember each other.

As for what the next world is like, if I am bold enough to speculate on holding to faith in the face of suffering and on the nature of a soul, then I might as well complete this speculation on the trilogy of last things.

Some time ago, Pope Benedict XVI surprised a few people when he suggested that heaven, hell, and purgatory may not be places where we do time, but could be experiences through which we arrive or pass. I think he is right, not only because time and space are elements of this imperfect world, not the next world, but also because this opens up interesting ideas about what these experiences might be like, and how rich the Catholic tradition is in this regard.

When I think of what the hereafter might be like, I turn by way of analogy to the magnificent parable of God's mercy in Luke 15:11—24, the Prodigal Son. Here is a Jewish boy who commits two of the worst sins he could commit: he squanders his patriarch's inheritance and is so down on his luck that he would have gladly eaten what the pigs are eating. Then he decides to go home and make up with his dad. I think that is what death is like for all of us, the final journey. This image is poignantly evoked in the final holy communion given to our dying, which is called the *Viaticum*, which literarily means food for the journey.

In the story, meanwhile, the father watches and waits on the road all day, every day, for any sign of the son's return. I think it is worth noting that the father did not go and club the son over the head and haul him home. The son had to put himself on the road home, which is similar to what happens when we die. We begin the final journey home. And when this extraordinary father sees him, he rushes out, kisses him, and calls for a party, and all this even before the kid has had a chance to finish his well-rehearsed apology. That has to be heaven. For some of us who do our best, though we also fail, we get the basics right, while God, who knows our heart and has accompanied us as we have labored under the difficulties with which we have lived, does not even want the apology. We are welcomed home.

However, for some of us, the meeting with God may be personally painful because, as I have argued throughout this book, God takes our free choices very seriously. So when the extraordinary Father sees some of us, he rushes out to meet us, but when we are face to face with love itself, we are aware of the many free and knowing times we have been destructive toward ourselves, others, and our world. At that point, we will be allowed to start and finish the well-rehearsed apology, asking, indeed in some cases, begging, for forgiveness. It will cost us dearly to own what we have done, because it will be so stark, and it will cost God to forgive us. But because the Father is full of mercy and compassion, we will be cleansed, or purged, in love. Echoes of this approach are found in Pope Benedict's words, "Today we are used to thinking: What is sin? God is great, he understands us, so sin does not count, in the end God will be good toward all....It's a nice hope. But there is justice, and there is real blame. Those who have destroyed man [sic] and the earth cannot sit immediately at the table of God, together with their victims."

Finally, I think there may be some of us who will make the journey home. The Father will rush to meet us, but when we are face to face with love itself, we will do what we have freely and knowingly chosen to do all our lives—we will reject God's love and walk away, the ultimate sin, which no doubt reflects how our lives on earth were spent. That has to be hell—the abyss—to see the face of God, of love itself, and walk away from it because we always have. And the Father painfully respects our choice, even this one to reject him. As the pope says, "...it is precisely the last judgment of God that guarantees justice....We must speak specifically of sin as the possibility of destroying oneself, and thus also other parts of the earth." But like the pope, I do not think this final group is large. "Perhaps there are not so many who have destroyed themselves so completely, who are irreparable forever, who no longer have any element upon which the love of God can rest, who no longer have the slightest capacity to love within themselves. This would be hell."

This is why I do not believe that God kills us off, but that as painful as death is, we know that we will see our brother or sister again, and that Christian hope says that our parting is not a definitive "goodbye," but more a "see you later."

CONCLUSION

Some might think that the theology outlined here presents God as remote or aloof. I do not need to think that God has to be the direct cause of everything in my life to have a strong and lively belief in a personal God. Indeed, I am passionate about God's personal love and presence. As stated throughout, thinking that God is removed from the intricate detail of how things develop does not remove God from the drama of our living, our suffering, and our dying.

God accompanies us at every moment of our short or long life. The word *accompany* here is a strong one. It can mean to attend someone actively, to be concomitant, to add and enrich, and to support (as in a musical accompaniment). Each meaning adds a layer of depth in regard to how God accompanies us in life and through death. I also like the fact that the word *accompany* is a Middle French corruption of the words companion and company, which are from the Latin words *com*, "with," and *panis*, "bread": *with one who breaks the same bread*. This incorporates the sense of solidarity—that "we are in it together" and defines Christian hope. God is in this with us, which is, of course, the story of the incarnation.

In her book *Metaphorical Theology: Models of God in Religious Language*, Sallie McFague outlines some new metaphors for our relationship with God, and of Jesus. Not all of the ones she outlines are compelling or appealing. However, one of them is God-as-friend. The reclaiming of that metaphor for my adult relationship with God, Christ, and the Spirit has had a major impact on me.

This image is appealing because we choose our friends and they choose us, we like to spend time with them, and we tell intimate things to our best friends that we tell to few others. Sometimes, when we are on top of the world or in a crisis, we may call our best friends even ahead of our families. And we know our friends like us because they seek us out and want to share our life. They accompany us throughout life, attending us, enriching, and supporting us. We experience friendship especially at meals, while breaking the same bread.

It is not childish to call God our friend, or to claim Jesus and the Spirit as our best friends. I think it is a particularly adult idea. Jesus is with us at every moment of life, especially when we wonder where the hell God has gone. Like all our friends who truly love us, God does not inflict pain, set out to punish us, or set up accidents to teach us lessons or make us grow. Although this unchanging, divine friend may be eternal, self-existent, transcendent, holy, and ever-present, God's love knows restraint, as the best love always does; a self-imposed restraint on his power and knowledge. Therefore, God does not send natural disasters or famines. God does not kill us off. In fact, this heavenly friend wants nothing to do with death. We know that because of what we see in Jesus. In him there is no darkness, only light, no retribution or revenge, no smiting of the enemy. There is a demand for justice but no reprisals. And Jesus did not enter our world to die but to live, and to be our Way, Truth, and Life. Just as Jesus was killed because of the way he lived, so, too, God's last word on Jesus' death was life, to raise his Son from the grave. As a result, this friend's will or plan for us is for us to flourish in faith, hope, and love as we realize all our gifts and talents.

Yet Christ-as-friend does not barge in. He waits patiently for an invitation to enter our lives at whatever level we want. Jesus meets us where we are, embraces us, and holds us close when the going gets tough, and helps us find the way forward, even on that last day when we find the way home.

SELECT BIBLIOGRAPHY

Cowburn, John. *Shadows and the Dark*. London: SCM, 1979.

——. *Predestination and Determinism*. Milwaukee, WI: Marquette University Press, 2008.

Doyle, Brian. *Leaping: Revelations and Epiphanies*. Chicago: Loyola Press, 2003.

Hick, John. *Evil and the God of Love*. London: Macmillan/Palgrave Press, 2007.

Leonard, Richard. *Preaching to the Converted on Sundays and Feast Days of the Year*. Mahwah, NJ: Paulist Press, 2006.

Leonard, Tracey. *The Full Catastrophe*. Mahwah, NJ: Paulist Press, 2010.

Martin, James. *The Jesuit Guide to (Almost) Everything: A Spirituality for Real Life*. New York: HarperOne, 2010.

McFague, Sallie. *Metaphorical Theology: Models of God in Religious Language*. Philadelphia: Fortress Press, 1982.

O'Sullivan, Patrick. *Prayer and Relationships: Staying Connected, An Ignatian Perspective*. Melbourne: David Lovell Publishing, 2008.

Wiesel, Elie. *Night*. New York: St. Martin's Press, 1995.